The

Tao Te Ching

Lao Tzu's Book of the Way and of Righteousness

Translation and Commentary

By

Charles Johnston

www.kshetrabooks.com

The Tao Teh King, An Interpretation of Lao Tse's Book of the Way and of Righteousness
Serialized in the *Theosophical Quarterly*, 1921-23

Tao Te Ching: Lao Tzu's Book of the Way and of Righteousness
1st Edition

ISBN: 978-1537196473

Introductory Article: The Religion of China

Theosophical Quarterly, January, 1907

The records of China go back nearly five thousand years. Twenty-eight centuries before our era, say these records, a hundred families, coming from the west, entered China as conquerors, gradually building up a kingdom, and then an empire. From these hundred families several successive dynasties arose, among whom certain monarchs gained enduring fame. The sacred books of ancient China record the sayings and doings of these monarchs, their wisdom and justice; and they are sacred through the reverence paid to the antique kings, rather than from any claim to inspiration, or from dealing with divine things. In truth they are histories and poems, rather than scriptures; yet the divine shines through them, and the view they give of life is lofty and noble, full of faith in God and immortality.

Some three or four centuries after the coming of the Hundred Families, a certain Exalted Lord ruled over the Kingdom of Flowers. His title was Ti Yao, and his history is enshrined in the earliest chapter of the *Shu King*, the ancient Chinese Book of Histories.[1] Of this monarch of the twenty-fourth century before our era, four thousand three hundred years ago, the *Shu King* says:

> "Examining into antiquity, we find that the Exalted Lord, Ti Yao, was reverential, intelligent, accomplished, and thoughtful,—naturally, and without effort. He was sincerely courteous, and capable of all complaisance. His bright influence was felt through the four quarters, and reached to heaven above, and earth beneath.

> "He distinguished the able and virtuous, and thence proceeded to the love of the nine classes of his kindred, who thus became harmonious. He also regulated and polished the people, who all became devoutly intelligent. He united and harmonized the myriad states, and so the black-haired people were transformed. The result was universal concord.

> "He commanded the brothers of the Hsi and Ho families in reverent accordance with the wide heavens to calculate and delineate the sun, the moon, the stars, and the zodiacal spaces, and so to deliver respectively the seasons to be observed by the people. He declared to the Hsi and Ho brothers that a round year consisted of three hundred and sixty and six days. . . ."

The exalted Yao thus played in China somewhat the same part as had been played in Egypt, some two thousand years earlier, by the great Menes, who "united the Two Lands" of Upper and Lower Egypt into a single stable monarchy. In due time, Yao desired to retire from his throne, and sought everywhere for a worthy successor. A certain Shun was recommended to him, of whom it was said: "his father was obstinately unprincipled, his step-mother was insincere, his half-brother was arrogant. But by his filial piety he has been able to live in harmony with them, and to lead them gradually to self-government." No stronger recommendation could be asked for, therefore Shun was sought out, and after due testing, was enthroned in Lord Yao's stead, "receiving Yao's retirement in the temple of the Accomplished Ancestor." Of Shun, the *Shu King* tells us that:

"He examined the pearl-domed turning sphere, with its transverse axle of jade, and reduced to a harmonious system the movements of the Seven Directors."

In this poetical way we are told that Shun, like his great predecessor, was an astronomer; for the pearl-adorned sphere is the proud overhanging firmament fretted with golden fire, and the Seven Directors are the Seven Stars, called in India the Seven Seers, and later the Great Bear. The *Shu King* continues concerning Lord Shun:

"Thereafter he sacrificed specially, but with ordinary forms, to God; sacrificed with reverent purity to the Six Honoured Ones; offered their appropriate sacrifices to the hills and rivers; and extended his worship to the host of spirits. He made a tour of inspection eastwards as far as Thai Tsung (in Shan-tung), where he presented a burnt offering to Heaven, and sacrificed in order to the hills and rivers. Thereafter he gave audience to the princes of the east. He set in accord their seasons and months, and regulated the days: he made uniform the standard tubes, with the measures of length and capacity, and the steel yards; he regulated the five ceremonies. ... He then returned to the capital, went to the temple of the Cultivated Ancestor, and sacrificed a single bull. ... He instituted the division of the land into twelve provinces, raising altars upon twelve hills in them. He also deepened the rivers. He exhibited to the people the statutory punishments ... and money to be received for redeemable offences ... Those who transgressed presumptuously and repeatedly were to be punished with death. 'Let me be reverent! Let me be reverent!' he said. 'Let compassion rule in punishment!'"

In due time, the Lord Shun "went on high and died." Of his successor Yü, it is said in the *Shu King*:

"On the first morning of the first month, he received the appointment in the temple dedicated by Shun to the spirits of his ancestors."

The *Shu King* records the following noble sentiments of another monarch of the same period:

"Heaven hears and sees as our people hear and see; Heaven rightly approves or displays its terrors as our people brightly approve or would awe; such connection is there between the upper and lower worlds. How reverent ought the masters of territories to be! ...

"To revere and honour the path prescribed by Heaven is the way ever to preserve the favouring appointment of Heaven."

It is related that, some three thousand six hundred years ago, the Lord Thang ruled over the Land of Flowers. To his princess he addressed these words, as the *Shu King* records:

"I am fearful and trembling, as if I were in danger of falling into a deep abyss. Throughout all the regions that enter on a new life under me, do ye not follow lawless ways; make no approach to insolence and dissoluteness; let every one be careful to keep his statutes; that so he may receive the favour of Heaven. The good in you I will not dare to keep consoled, and for the evil in me, I will not dare to forgive myself. I will examine these things in harmony with the mind of God."

This last magnificent sentence would be hard to parallel, in the sacred books of other faiths. It is full of the grandeur of simple piety and abiding faith in Providence; and it is characteristic of the ancient religion of China that all earthly events are viewed as immediate expressions of the Divine Will. "Good and evil do not wrongfully befall men," says the *Shu King*, "but Heaven sends down misery or happiness according to their conduct."

Another monarch of the same epoch declares:

"When I offer the great sacrifices to my predecessor, your forefathers are present to share in them. They all observe the happiness I confer and the sufferings I inflict, and I cannot dare to reward virtue that does not exist."

These passages give a fair view of the quality of the *Shu King*, with it pictures of Yao and Shun and Thang, and the ancient monarchs who ruled in reverence and virtue, sacrificing to God, to the Six Great Ones, to the Ancestors, to the spirit of river and hill. There is no theology here, but very genuine religion, and even more ethics. Religion is applied directly to life, to the social system; and the duties of all classes, from the king to the husbandman, are looked on as appointed by High Heaven, who rewards the righteous and punishes evil-doers. There is also a strong faith in immortality, in the survival of the spirit of the ancestor, who dwell close to their descendant, watching over them, and receiving from them the offerings at the four great sacrifices of spring, summer, autumn and winter. "When the lutes are strongly swept or gently touched," says the *Shu King*, "the progenitor of the Ruler come to the service."

The *Shih King*, the Book of Odes,[2] sheds a further light on these sacrifices to the Progenitor. Here is part of the Ode sung at the sacrifice offered to the Lord Thang, of whom we have already spoken:

"How admirable! How complete!
Here are set our cymbals and drums.
The drums resound harmonious and loud.
To delight our meritorious Ancestor!
The descendant of Thang invites him with his music,
That he may soothe us with the realization of our thought.
Deep is the sound of our cymbals and drums, shrilly sound the flutes,
All harmonious, and blending together.
According to the notes of the sonorous gem.
Oh majestic is the descendant of Thang;
Very admirable is his music
The large bells and drums, fill the ear;
The various dances are grandly performed.
We have the admirable visitors,
Who are pleased and delighted.

From of old, before our time,
The men of old set us the example,
How to be mild and humble from morning to night,
And to be reverent in discharging the service.
May he regard our sacrifice of winter and autumn,
Thus offered by the descendant of Thang!"

We see that the quarterly sacrifice to the spirits of the Ancestors was a kind of dramatic performance, with music and dancing, and a certain effect of orchestral richness. It was held in the temple of the Ancestors, and visitors were invited to take part in it. Sacrifices were offered, generally a red bull, and we learn that a liquor distilled from rice or millet was also poured out as a libation to the spirits of the ancestors.

One sentence in this Ode needs further consideration: that in which the spirit of Thang is asked to soothe his praying descendant with "a realization of his thought." This refers to the central event of the sacrifice, the apparition of the progenitor himself. The descendant who offered this sacrifice spent three days in fasting, during which he was to call up before his mind's eye the image of the progenitor to whom the offering was made, imaginatively reproducing every detail of his face and garments and gestures, until a living and moving picture was visible to his mind's eye. He was to carry this picture to the temple of the ancestors, and there the spirit of the ancestor would enter and vivify the form thus reproduced, communing with his descendant, and revealing to him secrets, or giving him wise counsel. The Book of Odes makes it clear that not only fathers and grandfathers were thus invoked, but that the spirits of women ancestors were likewise called on:

"Abundant is the year with much millet and rice;
And we have our high granaries,
With tens and hundreds of thousands, and millions of measures,
For liquors and sweet liquors,
To present to our ancestors male and female,
And to supply all our ceremonies.
The blessings sent down on us are of every kind."

Among the Odes of the *Shih King*, there are some full of pathos and aspiration; prayers in a very true sense. Such is the following, uttered by a servant of the state, who had been wrongfully accused and disgraced by the king:

"O vast and distant Heaven,
Who art called our Father!
That without crime or offence,
I should suffer from disorders thus great!
The terrors of great Heaven are excessive,
But indeed I have committed no crime.
The terrors of great Heaven are excessive,
But indeed I have committed no offence!"

Hardly less touching is the following prayer of a youthful prince called to reign before he had come to strength, and weighed down by the burden laid upon him:

"Alas for me, who am a little child,
On whom has devolved the unsettled state!
Solitary am I, and full of distress,
Oh my great father,
All thy life long thou wast filial,
Thou didst think of my great grandfather,
Picturing him ascending and descending, in the court,
I, the little child,
Day and night will be as reverent.
Oh, ye great kings!
As your successor,
I will strive not to forget you!"

Noteworthy all through the earlier Chinese books is the view that God removes dynasties as well as sets them up. There is the divine right of kings, so long as they rule justly. Then, when they fall from justice and virtue, a new dynasty is appointed, and rules equally by right divine. This doctrine is well illustrated in the following lines from one of the Major Odes of the *Shih King*:

"Great is God,
Beholding this lower world in majesty,
He surveyed the four quarters of the kingdom,
Seeking for someone to give establishment to the people.
Those two earlier dynasties
Had failed to satisfy Him with their government;
So throughout the various states,
He sought and considered
For one on whom He might confer the rule.
Hating all the great states,
He turned kind regards on the west,
And there gave a settlement. . . ."

It is a tribute to the essentially democratic spirit of ancient China, that the poem of the small farmer appears in the ancient Book of Odes, side by side with the memorial song of the departed king. It would be hard to find a more vivid expression of common life, the life of the toiling millions of men, than is enshrined in this poem:

"Very sharp are the excellent plough-shares
With which they set to work on the south-lying acres.
They sow their various kinds of grain,
Each seed containing in it a germ of life.
There are those who come to see them
With their baskets round and square,
Containing the provision of millet.
With their light splint hats on their heads,
They ply their hoes on the ground,
Clearing away the smartweed on dry land and wet,

The weeds being decayed,
The millet grows luxuriously.
The millet falls rustling before the reapers;
The gathered crop is piled up solidly,
High as a wall, united like the teeth of a comb;
And the hundred houses are open to receive it,
Those hundred houses being full,
The wives and children have a feeling of repose.
Now we kill the black-muzzled tawny bull.
With his crooked horns,
To imitate and hand down,
To hand down the observances of our ancestors."

There is a like natural freshness in this little poem, which is also very ancient:

"Crash! crash! respond the falling trees;
Chirp, chirp, respond the birds to their fellows.
They come from the shady delta
Flitting upon the lofty trees,
Answering each other in their songs.
And seeking their friends with their notes;
Behold these songsters!
Like friends they ask for replies.
Shall it be then that men
Desire not their living friends?
The gods listen to those
Who to their end are peaceful and united."

Even more pathetic is the following song of sorrow:

"Even the solitary larch
Has leaves to form a green shade;
But I must wander alone and forlorn.
Do I say there are no human beings?
No! But none to me is kindred.
Ah, ye who pass by,
Will none of you consort with me?
A man bereft of his brothers;
Alas! will none assist me?"

With these texts in mind, let us now take a general survey of the ancient religion of China. All the elements are included in the citations we have given from the oldest Sacred Books. We find, a the head and front of this ancient religion, a genuine reverence for God, the moral and intelligent Governor of the Universe, who is approached in prayer, who watches over mankind, exalting the humble and casting down the mighty from their seats. God is the author of moral law, of the law of righteousness; and he who would be righteous must act "in harmony with the mind of God." Very genuine virtues were recognized: honesty, humility, temperance, compassion, effective work for others; and there was a single standard for king and peasant alike. The realm of God is personified as Heaven; or perhaps it would be better to say that divine providence is so personified; yet God is always thought of as one and indivisible, mighty, and just.

Reverent worship is next paid to the hosts of spirits, also held to be intelligent and moral beings, dwelling in the invisible world, guiding the movements of the heavenly bodies, and the ordered processes of natural forces on earth. These spirits are the ministers of God, and carry out God's decrees throughout nature, and toward man.

Regular worship is also paid to the spirits of the dead, in sacrifices celebrated every quarter, or every year. Bulls and rams are offered as burnt offerings, and rice-wine and the liquor of millet are poured forth to them a libations. As far a these ancient books tell us, the condition of the spirits of the dead is uniformly happy. Where there has been sin, it has been punished by suffering on earth, and the spirits of ancestors are gathered in the realm of the divine, whence they watch over their descendants, and whence they come, summoned by music, to the festal sacrifices, to commune with their children and grandchildren, to counsel them, reproving or approving their works.

This is the entire spiritual content of the ancient Chinese religion, as shown in the most ancient Sacred Books of China. It is not less remarkable for what it contains than for what is omitted. It is a religion of light. There is no dark counterpart of the Deity, there are no gloomy Spirits of the Abyss. There is no hell of torment for erring mortals. Further, among the cardinal omissions we may reckon the fact that there is no cosmogony, no teaching of the Creation or Evolution of the worlds; there is no Deluge story; there is no system of Avatars, such as we find in nearly all religions; there is no doctrine of Reincarnation or rebirth. Among the spirits, we find those who punish evil-doing, but we find no spirits of malice and destruction.

We have seen that the Hundred Families came from the west some five thousand years ago, and settled on the Hoang-ho. It has been conjectured, with much show of reason, that they came from a region within the influence of the ancient Sumerians, whose land we may call Chaldea.[3] Like them, they had a hieroglyphic system, closely resembling that of ancient Egypt, and it is the difference of writing material, more than anything else, which has differentiated the Chinese ideographs from the Chaldean cuneiform. The worship of God as the Spirit of Heaven, the worship of the hosts of spirits, and of the souls of ancestors all take us toward Chaldea; yet we miss entirely in the Chinese system the dark and sinister elements so conspicuous in the Chaldean system, especially as developed at Nippur, in the north of the Chaldean land. The numeral and astronomical systems of China also point toward Chaldea, and nearly all our Sinologues are ready to accept these indications. Yet it seems difficult to account for the omissions just pointed out. How is it that the Chinese have preserved the light of Chaldea without the shadow? Are we not almost forced to believe that the Chinese and Chaldean systems are divergent branches of a common source, in some region further to the north, perhaps in the neighbourhood of Issyk Kul, and that from this centre colonies went forth in three directions, to the Euphrates valley, to the headwaters of the Indus, to the Hoang-ho, carrying with them the worship of God as the Spirit of Heaven; of the hosts of spirits; of the souls of the departed, who were propitiated and nourished by regular sacrifices, in Chaldea, in India and in China alike?

In each case, these colonies of many thousand years ago came into contact with older populations, who already possessed strongly contrasted elements of religion. Thus in Chaldea the ancestor-worshippers were mingled with an Egyptian colony, worshippers of Osiris, whom they reverenced as a divine Incarnation. In India, the ancestor-worshippers found the more ancient Rajanya or Rajput race, akin to the Egyptians, and in possession of the Mystery Teaching which was the secret splendour of Egypt. In China, the ancestor-worshippers were mingled with older tribes, of older races, for whom the propitiation of demons was a large part of religion, as it was also with a part of the population of Chaldea and among the darker races of southern India. Thus grew up the later deformation of a purer primitive faith.

II.

When we come to the Chinese sages, of whom Lao Tzu is the most renowned, we find many of the elements which are missing in the older religion of China. Here are cosmogonies, accounts of the Creation of the world; and here also are more mystical elements, making a closer approach to what we have found in Egypt and India.

In the works of the great sage Yü Tze, who was at the height of his fame rather more than three thousand years ago, we find certain of these mystical elements. When asked by his disciple King Wen-Wang what was the supreme shortcoming, the sage replied:

"To know one's faults, and not to correct them. Acting thus, a man loses himself, and destroys his own life. This is the ruin of the principles of government and morals. The righteous man and the sinful man are shown by their words and deeds. Thus he who rejects error, knows the truth; he who hates evil, follows good. Thus wisdom (Tao) is in his speech. The teaching which has been handed down to our day, and which gives happiness to the world, is what is called Tao. Sincere benevolence is what brings the people what they need, without their seeking. To drive away the evils of this world is the work of goodness. Goodness and loyalty, peace and justice (Tao) are the principles of action of sovereigns; all beings are the instruments of these principles. He who ignores them, will not attain his end."

From the same sage, who preceded Lao Tzu by five centuries, we quote also a fragment of cosmogony:

"Heaven-and-Earth brought forth, and all beings were born. All beings thus born were governed by man. He can slay what he has not brought to life; but what Heaven-and-Earth have slain, he cannot bring to life. Man changes to grow better. Animals change only to become worse. A man whose acts are evil is justly called an animal.

"There was first Heaven, then Earth. When the Earth was formed, distinction immediately came into being. From distinction came right and duty. After right and duty came the teaching, and after the teaching, the body of principles. From the principles came the rules of action, and then the numbers were formed.

"The sun has its darkness and its brightness, the day and night, and this produces numbers. The moon waxes and wanes, and has its conjunctions and disjunctions, which mark the periods. These four facts by their fixity rule the numbers."

Contemporary with this sage was another, Tze-Ya-Tze by name, also a preceptor of King Wen-Wang. When the monarch was at the point of death he called his heir, and asked the sage to declare the principles of Tao, the teaching of wisdom. The sage replied:

"Three things hinder Tao: to see the good to be done, and to neglect it; to hesitate when the occasion presents itself; and to know evil and follow it. On the other hand, four things make Tao prosper: perfect calm with gentleness; respect with diligence in duty; humility with force; firmness with endurance."

The words of these two sages have this added interest, that they show us the use of the mysterious word Tao several centuries before it was chosen by the great Lao Tzu as the central thought of his great work the *Tao Te Ching:* "the Book of Tao and Te," "of the Way and Virtue."

Lao Tzu was born in the year 604 B.C., in the third year of King Ting of the Chan dynasty. He was curator of the royal library of Chan, but filled with grief over the decadence of the dynasty he determined to retire from the world and betake himself to the mountain region to the west of China. At the pass on the frontier, in Honan, he was recognized by the guardian of the pass, himself a lover of wisdom, who asked him to leave a record of his doctrine. This record is the *Tao Te Ching*, divided into two parts, and containing five thousand characters. It contains eighty-one short chapters, sentences from some of which we shall give:[4]

"The way that can be trodden is not the enduring and unchanging Way. The word that can be named is not the enduring and unchanging Word.

"Having no name, It is the originator of Heaven and Earth; having a name, It is the Mother of all things.

"Under these two aspects It is really the same; but as development proceeds, It receives different names. Together we call them the Mystery. Where the Mystery is deepest, is the gate of all that is subtle and wonderful." (1: 1, 2, 4)

It is evident that the Tao of Lao Tzu is Brahma or Atma of the Upanishads, described as "the Living Self, the great Mother, full of divinity, who comes forth through life, standing hid in secret, born through creatures."[5] In Chinese, Tao has three meanings: in the physical sense, it is a Way; in the moral sense, it is Wisdom; in the spiritual sense, it is the Oversoul, the Eternal, the Logos. Let us quote further:

"Tao is like the emptiness of a vessel; and in our employment of It, we must be on our guard against all fullness How deep and unfathomable it is, as if It were the honoured Ancestor of all things!

"We should blunt our sharp points, and unravel the complications of things; we should temper our brightness, and bring ourselves into agreement with the obscurity of others. How pure and still the Way (Tao) is, as if It would ever so continue.

"I do not know whose son It is. It might appear to have been before God." (4: 1, 2, 3.)

With this we may compare the words of the Upanishad:

"When the five perceptions and mind are steadied; and when the soul struggles not, this, they say, is the highest Way. . . . All that the universe is, moves in life, emanated from It."[6]

Once more Lao Tzu:

"Heaven is long-enduring, and Earth continues long. The reason why Heaven and Earth are able to endure and continue thus long, is because they do not live of, or for, themselves.

"Therefore the Sage puts his own person last, and yet it is found in the foremost place; he treats his person as if it were foreign to him, and yet that person is preserved. Is it not because he has no personal and private ends, that therefore such ends are realized?" (7: 1, 2.)

Here again, we may compare the Upanishad teaching:

"Considering the life of the powers as apart, and their rising and setting a they grow up apart, the Sage grieves not. . . . When all desires that dwell in the heart are let go, the mortal becomes immortal."[7]

We may also compare the words of another Teacher:

"The last shall be first, and the first, last."[8]

The *Tao Te Ching* further declares:

"The highest excellence is like water. The excellence of water appears in its benefiting all things, and in its occupying, without striving, the low place which all men dislike. Hence its way is nearer to that of Tao." (8: 1.)

This vividly recalls the words of St. Francis of Assisi:

"Praised be my Lord for our sister water, who is very serviceable unto us, and humble and precious and clean."[9]

Once more from the *Tao Te Ching*:

"When the intelligent and animal souls are held together in one embrace, they can be kept from separating. When one gives undivided attention to the life, and brings it to the utmost degree of pliancy, he can become as a babe. When he has cleansed away the most mysterious sights, he can become without a flaw. . . .

"Tao produces all things and nourishes them; It produces them and does not claim them a Its own: It does all, and yet does not boast of it; It presides over all things, and yet does not dominate them. This is what is called the Mysterious Quality of Tao." (10: 1.)

The first part of this passage teaches that the animal soul must be held firmly in subjection to the divine soul; that thus the life-force will be concentrated, and perfect control reached; that the mind-images in the psychic body must be purified; that thus the disciple will become as a little child, pure and without flaw. The purity from egotism thus reached is illustrated by the Soul, which, having made all things, boasts not. Lao Tzu continues:

"We look at It, and we do not see It, and we name it 'the Equable.' We listen to It, and we do not hear It, and we name It 'the Inaudible.' We try to grasp It, and we do not get hold of It, and we name It 'the Subtle.' With these three qualities, It cannot be made the subject of description; hence we blend them, and obtain 'the One.'" (14: 1.)

Compare with this the Upanishad teaching.

"The form of That does not stand visible, nor does anyone behold It with the eye. By the heart, the soul, the mind, It is grasped; and those who know It, become immortal."[10]

This is, no doubt, the real meaning of the oft quoted saying that Tao promotes longevity, generally misunderstood in a bodily sense.

"The subtle Masters (of Tao) in olden times, with a subtle and exquisite penetration, comprehended its mysteries, and were deep also, so as to elude men's knowledge." (15: 1.)

"The partial becomes complete; the crooked, straight; the empty, full; the worn-out, new; he whose desires are few, gets them; he whose desires are many, goes astray.

"Therefore the Sage holds in his embrace humility, and manifests it to all the world. He is free from self-display, and therefore he shines; from self-assertion, and therefore he is distinguished; from self-boasting, and therefore his merit is acknowledged; from self-complacency, and therefore he acquires superiority. It is because he is thus free from striving that therefore no one in the world is able to strive with him." (22: 1, 2.)

Perhaps these sentences show better than any others that Lao Tzu is in truth one of the Illumined, and that his teaching is the immemorial wisdom of old, the wisdom that the Seers know.

"There was something undefined and complete, coming into existence before Heaven and Earth. How still It was and formless, standing alone, and undergoing no change, reaching everywhere and inexhaustible. It may be regarded as the Mother of all things.

"I do not know its name, and I give It the designation of Tao. Making an effort to give It a name, I call It the Great.

"Being Great, It passes on. Passing on, It becomes remote. Having became remote, It returns. Therefore Tao is great; Heaven also is great, Earth is great; and the royal Sage is great. In the universe there are four things that are great, and the royal Sage is one of them.

"Man takes his law from the Earth; the Earth takes its law from Haven; Heaven takes its law from Tao. The law of Tao is being what It is." (25: 1, 2, 3, 4.)

This is the teaching of Emanation, thus set forth in the Upanishad:

"The Lord of Beings desired beings. He brooded with fervour; and, brooding with fervour, he forms a pair. These are the Substance and the Life. 'These two will make beings manifold for me,' said he."[11]

This is almost verbally the same as the sentence of Lao Tzu:

"Tao produced One; One produced Two; Two produced Three; Three produced all things." (42: 1.)

"To those who are good, I am good; and to those who are not good, I am also good. To those who are sincere, I am sincere; and to those who are not sincere, I am also sincere." (49: 2.)

The closest parallel to this is found, perhaps, in the words:

"Ye have heard that it hath been said, Thou shalt love thy neighbour, and hate thine enemy. But I say unto you, Love your enemies, bless them that curse you, do good to them that hate you, and pray for them which despitefully use you and persecute you; that you may be the children of your Father which is in heaven; for he maketh his sun to rise on the evil and on the good, and sendeth rain on the just and the unjust."[12]

"Tao which originated all under the sky is to be considered the Mother of them all.

"When the Mother is found, we know what her children should be. When one knows that he is his Mother's child, and proceeds to guard the qualities of the Mother that belong to him, to the end of his life he will be free from all peril." (52: 1.)

This beautiful passage is most closely paralleled by that quoted already from the Upanishads, concerning "the great Mother, full of divinity, who comes forth through life;" and we find the same image in another Upanishad:

"All this is in Life's sway, all that is set firm in the triple heaven. Guard us as a Mother her sons, and as fortune, give us wisdom!"[13]

The closest approach to this personification of divine Wisdom as the Mother to be found in the New Testament is, perhaps, the sentence of St. Paul to the Corinthians, where he speaks of the Christos as "*Theou dunamin kai Theou Sophian*,"[14] Sophia being taken as the feminine power of the Logos, the Sanskrit Vach. The primordial Mother in Sanskrit is called Aditi, from whom Ten Sons are born, the Host we might call them, of Planetary Spirits.[15]

"He who knows It, does not speak. He who is ready to speak, does not know It." (61: 1.)

This is exactly the same as the Upanishad sentence:

"Of whom It is not thought, of him It is understood; who thinks It, knows It not. It is unknown to the knowing; It is known to the unknowing."[16]

For this is the wisdom hid from the wise and prudent, and revealed to "babes"; the intuitional wisdom, which eludes the mind.

"The Master of Tao anticipates things that are difficult, while they are easy, and does things that would become great, while they are small. All difficult things in the world are sure to arise from a previous state in which they were easy, and all great things from one in which they were small. Therefore the Sage, while he never does what is great is able on that account to accomplish the greatest things." (63: 2.)

"The Sage desires what other men do not desire, and does not prize things difficult to get; he learns what other men do not learn, and turns back to what the multitude of men have passed by. Thus he helps the natural development of all things, and does not dare to act from his own desires." (64: 4.)

We may parallel this ideal from the Upanishads:

"The Self-being pierced the openings of the senses outward; hence one looks outward, not within himself. A wise man looked toward the Self with reverted sight, seeking immortality."[17]

We may close our study of Lao Tzu with these words:

"The Sage does not accumulate. The more he expends for others, the more does he possess of his own; the more he gives to others, the more he has for himself.

"With all the sharpness of the Way of Heaven, It injures not; with all the doing in the Way of the Sage, he does not strive." (81: 1, 3.)

The quotations suffice to show that Lao Tzu is a genuine Seer and Sage, worthy to be counted among the Wise Men of the world. His teaching is at all points in harmony with the teaching of the Upanishads, the Mystery Doctrine, and it is in such a work as the *Tao Te Ching* that we have the clearest evidence of the presence of the Mystery Teaching in China. It is true that in that Far-Eastern land the Mystery Teaching is rather a method, a Way, than a philosophy with ordered doctrines. Yet this is wholly in harmony with the spirit of that race and land, and is what we should look to find. It is worth remembering that Krishna speaks of himself as "the Way;" and that the method of that other Teacher who also said: "I am the Way," was called "the Way" before it was called the Gospel.

III.

A word in conclusion. The ancient Chinese religion which we have described and quoted, was gathered from many sources, and set in order by the great Confucius, who was born some fifty years later than Lao Tzu, and who knew that great Teacher. Confucius said of himself that he was a transmitter and not a maker, "one who believed in and loved the ancients;" and it was said of him that "he handed down the doctrines of Yao and Shun, as if they had been his ancestors." We have already seen what were the doctrines of Yao and Shun; amongst them was the reverence for ancestors here alluded to.

It is usual, in studies of the religions of China, to include an account of Buddhism, which reached that country in the sixtieth year of our era. I have thought it better to illustrate only what China herself contributes to the world's religions, omitting what other lands contributed to the religions of China.

Notes

1. The *Shujing* (simplified Chinese: 书经; traditional Chinese: 書經), variously translated as the "Book of Documents", the "Book of History", etc.. Tradition attributes its compilation to Confucius. The quotations used in this article appear to be drawn from James Legge's 1879 translation (*Sacred Books of the East*, Vol. 3), with Johnston's own modifications.

2. The *Shijing* (Chinese: 詩經), variously translated as the "Classic of Poetry", "Book of Songs", "Book of Odes", etc.. Tradition attributes its compilation to Confucius. The quotations used in this article appear to be drawn from James Legge's 1879 translation (*Sacred Books of the East*, Vol. 3), with Johnston's own modifications.

3. The present article was originally published in the *Theosophical Quarterly* (January, 1907), as the last installment of a four-part series, including: "The Religion of Ancient Egypt", January, 1906; "The Religion of Chaldea", April, 1906 and "The Religion of India", July, 1906.

4. This article was published a full 14 years prior to Johnston's complete translation of the *Tao Te Ching*. The selections included in the article represent Johnston's earliest effort of translation, and thus differ in wording from the full translation included in this volume.

5. *Katha Upanishad*, II:1:7

6. *Katha Upanishad*, II:3:10 & II:3:2

7. *Katha Upanishad*, II:3:6 & II:3:14

8. Matthew 20:16

9. *The Canticle of the Sun*, also known as the *Laudes Creaturarum* (Praise of the Creatures), by Saint Francis of Assisi, 1224.

10. *Katha Upanishad*, II:3:9

11. *Prashna Upanishad*, I:4

12. Matthew 5:43-45

13. *Prashna Upanishad*, II:13

14. Lit. "Divine power (or strength/might) and Divine wisdom." See 1 Corinthians 1:24. Johnston provides the Greek, which in full reads: "autois de tois klêtois ioudaiois te kai ellêsin christon theou dunamin kai theou sophian." In the King James Version, the translation is given as: "But unto them which are called, both Jews and Greeks, Christ the power of God, and the wisdom of God."

15. For more on these ideas see: H.P. Blavatsky, *The Secret Doctrine* (1888)

16. *Kena Upanishad*, II:3

17. *Katha Upanishad*, II:1

The Tao Te Ching

I

The way that can be told is not the eternal Way. The word that can be spoken is
  not the eternal Word.

Unnamed, It is the source of heaven and earth. Named, It is the Mother of all
  things.

He who is ever without desires sees Its spiritual essence. He who is ever under
  desire sees only Its limits.

These two, differing in name, are the same in origin. They are the mystery of
  mysteries. This is the door of spiritual life.

The eternal Way, Tao, is the Logos,[1] and was so rendered by the first translators of this
text. In the older Shu-King is the sentence: "Let us learn all things in harmony with the
Mind of God"; the Logos being the Mind of God, as well as the Word of God.

The Logos has two aspects: unnamed, and named; the unmanifest and the manifested
Logos. From the manifested Logos comes the visible universe, the unity of heaven and
earth. Heaven means here the immortal sea of spiritual consciousness; earth is the realm of
manifested nature.

Desires, the innumerable attachments to the things of manifested nature, bind the
consciousness to external things. Freedom from these multiplied attachments sets the
consciousness free to return to its home in the sea of immortal consciousness. Yet spiritual
consciousness and visible nature are not antagonistic; for nature is the garment of spiritual
consciousness, the Word made manifest in external life. Therefore he who relinquishes
attachment to external nature finds his way to the spiritual consciousness which is the Life
behind nature. He finds the Way, the door of spiritual life.

2

When all men have learned the beauty of righteousness, the ugliness of sin is
  understood.

When all men recognize goodness, then evil is understood.

In the same way, the manifest and the unmanifest define each other

Difficult and easy define each other

Long and short reveal each other

Height and depth manifest each other

Musical notes and the tones of the voice determine each other

Former and latter define each other

Therefore the Master works without working.

He teaches in silence.

Then all things come into being, and he gives them fruition.
He brings them into being, yet seeks not to possess them.
He perfects them, yet seeks no reward.
When his work is accomplished, he remains detached from it.
He seeks no glory, and is therefore glorious.

Lao Tzu is seeking to make clear the relation of the unmanifested and the manifested Logos to each other, as poles of the same Being. Spirit and matter are neither separated nor antagonistic; they are two aspects of the One. While the One is undivided, it remains unrevealed. Only by differentiation, by polarization into Spirit and matter, are the supplementary natures of Spirit and matter made apparent.

This, Lao Tzu makes clear by similes: beauty and ugliness make each others' nature manifest; righteousness and sin bring each other into clear relief. Long and short, high and low, define each other. So Spirit and matter, subject and object, perceiving consciousness and what is perceived, define each other.

Spirit is the positive, matter the negative pole. The Master, he who has relinquished all attachments to the things of matter, he whose consciousness has returned to the immortal sea of consciousness, thereafter works with Spirit. As Spirit works unseen, behind the veil of matter, so he works. As the divine Word teaches in silence, so he teaches. The laws of the working of Spirit are manifested in everything he does. Like Spirit, he is creative; like Spirit, he seeks no personal reward. Like the hidden Spirit, he seeks no glory; therefore, like the hidden Spirit, he is eternally glorious.

3

The seclusion of the Masters keeps the world from strife.
A low esteem of wealth keeps the world from covetousness.
When objects of desire are hidden, men's hearts are undisturbed.
Therefore, where the Master rules, he empties the heart of desires.
   He fills the inner nature. He strengthens its bones.
He constantly stills the mind and abates desires.
Those who have knowledge, he restrains from bondage to action.
He himself stands free from bondage to action; therefore all whom he rules
   abide in quietude.

It would appear that Lao Tzu consistently uses the similitude of the king and the kingdom in exactly the sense of the New Testament: the divine kingdom, the kingdom of heaven. The phrase for the kingdom, the empire, in the original: "that which is under heaven," makes still clearer the already transparent meaning.

The ruler of the kingdom is the Master; the kingdom consists of those who, loving the Master, obey him, rejoicing in his rule.

Without doubt, Lao Tzu has also in mind the ideal government of an earthly kingdom. There is no contradiction in this. The ideal for an earthly kingdom is, that it should be governed by a Master; that the divine will should be done "as in heaven, so on earth." Only then can the kingdom come.

But the time is not yet come. It can only come through general obedience to spiritual law. While rebellion against divine law is rife, the coming of a Master brings only strife and hostility. Therefore the seclusion of the Masters keeps the world from strife.

Lao Tzu again makes this clear by similes: When wealth is exposed to those whose hearts are full of greed, covetousness is fanned into flame. In exactly the same way, the coming of the Master to a world full of evil and rebellion, inflames evil and rebellion. Therefore a Master has said: "If I had not come, they had not had sin."[2]

But, even though not publicly recognized, the Master has his kingdom, in the hearts of his disciples. There he rules, emptying their hearts of desire. He enriches the inner nature, and builds the frame of the spiritual man. He stills the material mechanism of that mind which has been formed to "think matter." As the intelligence of his disciples awakens, he teaches them to keep their hearts free from bondage to action, from the thirst for personal reward; he makes clear to them that their right is to the action, but not to the personal reward; not to the result, as it may feed and flatter the lower self in them. And he has the power thus to rule and teach, because he himself stands free from bondage to action; therefore all whom he rules, his disciples, abide in quietude of heart; toiling in his work, but for the work's sake, without thought of personal reward.

4

The Way seems empty. As it is tried, it is found inexhaustible.
Oh, how profound it is! It seems to be the Forefather of all beings.
It quiets impetuosity. It looses bonds. It tempers its splendour.
  It follows lowliness.
Oh, how pure it is! It seems to abide for ever.
It is the Son of I-know-not. It seems to have been before the
  Lord of Heaven.

The carnal mind, says Saint Paul, is enmity against God.[3] Therefore, to the carnal mind, the mind full of desire, bound by innumerable appetites and attachments to carnal things, the Way appears not merely empty; it is altogether invisible.

But when, through the revulsion from carnal things, the little spark in the heart begins to seek and to find the Way, then it is found to be an infinite Way, whose treasures are inexhaustible.

The Way is the Life; not a static, arrested Life, but Life moving ever from glory to glory; therefore it is called the Way. And this Life, which ceaselessly progresses toward new splendours, is the Forefather of all beings.

When the Life and the Light take up their dwelling in the heart made empty of desires, impetuous desire is stilled. The bonds of attachment to the things of desire are loosed. The captive heart is made free. But the infinite Light does not shine forth in full radiance in the beginning, to dazzle and blind the eyes of the disciple. Its splendour is tempered for his growing sight, while that sight is yet dim. The Way is the way of humility.

As the Way is followed, it is found to be the path of all purification; it reveals itself as the eternal Way.

As the unmanifested Logos, the Way is the First-born of the Unknowable, Son of the hidden Father. From the unmanifested Logos spring the creative Powers; therefore it antecedes the Lord of Heaven.

5

Heaven and earth are without partiality. They regard all creatures as the dog (of
    straw in the sacrifice).
The Master is without partiality. He regards mankind as the dog
    of straw.
The Being that is between heaven and earth is like the bellows of the forge,
    empty, yet possessing power. Put in motion, it sends forth more and more.
He who would tell the Way, soon becomes silent.
It is better to follow the way of work with detachment.

The straw dogs are placed on the altar, to ward off evil. They are honoured with gifts. But, when the sacrifice is ended, they are thrown away.

Lao Tzu takes this as a symbol of impartiality. Heaven and earth are impartial, giving sun and rain alike to the just and the unjust. So the Master is impartial, without predilection, without favouritism, giving his life for the just and the unjust.

The same high virtue of impartiality, which is ideal justice, is enjoined by the *Bhagavad Gita*:

"He who is free from over-fondness, from partiality, meeting glory and gloom alike, who exults not nor hates, his perception is set firm."[4]

And the same impartiality is taught in another way by the Western Master:

"Then one said unto him, Behold, thy mother and thy brethren stand without, desiring to speak with thee. But he answered and said unto him that told him, Who is my mother? and who are my brethren? And he stretched forth his hand toward his disciples, and said, Behold my mother and my brethren! For whosoever shall do the will of my Father which is in heaven, the same is my brother, and sister, and mother."[5]

Since heaven and earth, Spirit and matter, are the two poles of the manifested world, that world itself is the Being between them; at first, before the beginning of Time, still and motionless; then, when the dawn comes, gradually stirred into manifestation.

But the divine Way, the Way of divine things, is so full of infinities, that he who seeks to tell it in words, is soon reduced to silence.

Better than words, to reveal the Way, is the following of the Way itself, by the path of disinterested obedience, the path of work without attachment.

Perhaps the best description of that path is to be found in the second book of the *Bhagavad Gita*, just quoted:

"Thy right is to the work, but never to its fruits of personal reward; let not the fruit of thy work be the motive, nor yet take refuge in abstinence from works.

"Standing in union with the Soul, carry out thy work, putting away attachment,

O conqueror of wealth; equal in success and failure, for equalness is called union with the Soul."[6]

But the principle of detachment, of high disinterestedness in work, is the main theme of the *Bhagavad Gita*, running through it all like a thread of gold. And in this principle of detachment, the Gita most closely approaches Lao Tzu's teaching.

6

The spirit of the valley dies not. It is called the mysterious Mother.
The door of the mysterious Mother is called the source of heaven and earth.
It is eternal and seems to manifest itself.
He who enters into it, finds rest.

The spirit of the valley is Humility. For only through humility is it possible to find the Way. The whole personality must be dissolved. The nothingness of self must be realized through and through, in will as well as in thought, before the light from within can illumine the heart.

When through humility the Way is found, it is found that the Power of the Way is the Life and source of all things. The mysterious Mother is called in India the feminine Viraj, or Vach,[7] the feminine aspect of the Logos; that which Saint Paul calls the Wisdom of God and the Power of God;[8] namely, God's power to make things manifest. This mysterious Mother, this formative Power, is eternal, and seems to manifest itself; the manifestation is a seeming, in the sense that it is not eternal. For only the Eternal is, in the fullest sense, real. All that is put forth in manifestation, will, in the fullness of time, be withdrawn from manifestation. He who would find rest, must seek it, not in manifested things, but in the Life which is behind manifested things, in the Logos, which, in all spiritual scriptures, is called the everlasting Home.

7

Heaven and earth endure.
If they endure, it is because they live not for themselves. It is because of this that they endure.
So the Master puts himself after others, yet remains the first.
He is detached from his body, yet conserves his body.
Is it not because he has no desires for himself, that all his desires are fulfilled?

Again, the teaching of high disinterestedness, of detachment from the desire of personal reward. Heaven and earth are impartial, sending sun and rain upon the just and the unjust. Heaven and earth are free from self-seeking, and therefore they endure for ever. The Master is, like the great Life which breathes through heaven and earth, impartial and free from self-seeking. Therefore let the disciple also be rid of all the wills of self.

8

The spirit of goodness is like water.
Water excels in doing good to all, yet strives not.
It seeks the lowly places rejected by others.
Therefore he who is like this, draws near to the Way.
His chosen dwelling place is in humility.
His heart loves the depth of the abyss.
His gifts are given with impartial love.
He speaks words of faithfulness.
His government brings peace.
He is skilful in all he undertakes.
He acts in all things with timeliness.
He strives against none; therefore he is not opposed.

The most fitting commentary on Lao Tzu's words concerning water, and, in general, what he says of the beneficence of heaven and earth, is the hymn of Saint Francis of Assisi, called the "Praises of the Creatures," more generally known as "The Canticle of the Sun." The quotation which follows is taken from the translation which Father Paschal Robinson has made from the earliest Italian manuscripts:

"Praise be to Thee, my Lord, with all Thy creatures,
Especially to my worshipful brother sun,
The which lights up the day, and through him dost
Thou brightness give;
And beautiful is he and radiant with splendour great;
Of Thee, most High, signification gives.
Praised be my Lord, for sister moon and for the stars,
In heaven Thou hast formed them clear and precious and fair.
Praised be my Lord for brother wind
And for the air and clouds and fair and every kind of weather,
By the which Thou givest to Thy creatures nourishment.
Praised be my Lord for sister water,
The which is greatly helpful and humble and precious and pure.
Praised be my Lord for brother fire,
By the which Thou lightest up the dark.
And fair is he and gay and mighty and strong.
Praised be my Lord for our sister, mother earth,
The which sustains and keeps us
And brings forth diverse fruits with grass and flowers bright.
Praised be my Lord for those who for Thy love forgive
And weakness bear and tribulation. . . ."

Here we have exactly the thought of the likeness between water, which is greatly helpful and humble and precious and pure, and those who, for love, forgive and bear weakness and tribulation, which Lao Tzu had expressed seventeen or eighteen centuries before Saint Francis.

9

It is better not to fill the vessel than to try to carry it when quite full.
The blade that is over-sharpened loses its edge, even though it be tested with the
    hand.
The hall that is filled with gold and jade cannot be guarded.
He who has honours heaped upon him, and thereby grows proud, draws down
    misfortune upon himself.
He who has done great things and gained renown should withdraw himself.
Such is the Way of heaven.

These vivid parables instilling moderation and humility hardly need any comment. The last phrase but one is thus interpreted by one of the Oriental commentators:

"When a hero has accomplished great things and gained renown, let him realize that life is like the illusion of a dream, that riches and honours are like floating clouds. When his time comes, he must let slip the bonds of the heart, escaping from his earthly prison, and, rising above creatures, become one with the Way."

10

The spiritual should rule the psychic nature.
When he is one-pointed, these act in consonance.
When he masters the bodily powers, rendering them obedient,
    he is as one new born.
When he frees himself from the illusions of the mind,
    he puts away all infirmities.
If he would guard the people and bring peace in the kingdom,
    let him work with detachment.
When he accepts the opening and closing of the gates of heaven,
    he rests like a brooding bird.
Though his light penetrates everywhere,
    he appears as if knowing nothing.
He brings forth beings and nourishes them.
Though bringing them forth, he is without the desire of possession.
He cherishes them, yet looks for no reward.
He rules them, yet without dominating them.
This is called perfect righteousness.

Here again very little comment is needed, though it may be of interest once more to quote an Oriental commentator:

"The nature of the holy man is serene and at rest, the spiritual part of his being is invariably set firm, and is not drawn awry nor perverted by material things. Although the spiritual soul has taken the animal soul for its abode, yet the animal soul obeys it in all that it undertakes. The spiritual principle commands and directs the animal principle. The men of the multitude subject their natures to external things, their hearts are troubled, and then the spiritual soul is dominated by the animal soul. Lao Tzu teaches men to hold the spirit firm, to rule the sensible nature, so that these two act together."

II

Thirty spokes unite in the nave. The use of the car depends on the empty space for the axle.

Clay is fashioned into vessels. The use of the vessels depends on the empty space within.

Doors and windows are framed in making a house. The use of the house depends on their empty spaces.

Therefore utility depends on what is manifest, but the use of a thing depends on what is unmanifest.

The point which Lao Tzu wishes to make appears to be that, while the material universe presents itself to our senses as stable and solid, its whole life depends upon immanent Spirit, the Logos, the vital stream which he calls the Way, and which, in itself is not manifest to the senses.

The same general thought is expressed by Paul, following Philo and Plato:

"The invisible things of him from the creation of the world are clearly seen, being understood by the things that are made, even his eternal power and Godhead."[9]

To put the same thought in a more modern way: Matter is useful because of the force which is manifested through it, and force is useful because of the yet more unmanifest Spirit which inwardly guides it.

But Lao Tzu has in mind also a direct application to conduct: The heart must be made empty of desires, in order that the Spirit of the Way may enter and possess it. Then only the life comes to its true use.

12

The five colours blind the eyes of men.

The five tones deafen the ears of men.

The five tastes deceive the mouths of men.

Impetuous motion, the passion of pursuit, madden the hearts of men.

The desire of possessions goads men to injurious acts.

Therefore the holy man is concerned with what is within, and not with the desire of the eyes.

Therefore he renounces what is without and cleaves to what is within.

The five colours, as enumerated by the Chinese commentator, are: red, blue, yellow, white and black. To the five notes of the scale, Chinese names are given. The five tastes are: sweet, sharp, acid, salt and bitter.

Lao Tzu is preaching a little sermon, not so much on the illusions of the five senses, as on fascination through the five senses. Perhaps the quaintest of all the sermons on this theme is found in one of the tracts attributed to Sankaracharya: "Beguiled by the five senses, five creatures meet with death, the deer, elephant, moth, fish and bee."[10] The deer is lured by music; the elephant is killed while ecstatically rubbing his head against a tree; the moth drawn to the flame is a universal simile; the fish is lured by the bait; the bee, attracted by the scent of the flower, is eaten by birds. The Sanskrit text draws the moral: "What, then, of man, allured by all the senses at once?"

The truth, in the larger philosophical sense, would seem to be that the outward-looking senses had their part in guiding us into manifested life. But the tide has turned; we should be on our homeward way. Therefore we must turn back, and look within. There we shall find the Way, leading us homeward.

13

The wise man shuns fame equally with infamy. His body weighs him down like a
   great misfortune.
What mean the words: He shuns fame equally with infamy?
There is something base in fame. To have it, is to be full of apprehension; to lose
   it, is to be full of apprehension.
Therefore it is said: He shuns fame equally with infamy. What mean the words:
   His body weighs him down like a great misfortune?
If we suffer great misfortunes, it is because we have bodies.
When we no longer have bodies, what misfortunes can we suffer?
Therefore, when a man shrinks from governing the kingdom,
   he may be trusted to govern the kingdom;
   when he is unwilling to govern the kingdom,
   he is fit to govern the kingdom.

Here again, the lesson is detachment. Attachment to the body, a perpetual gratification of the appetites of the body, causes most of the maladies of the body. But the body used as the soul's instrument, not pampered and indulged, is full of vigour.

So the vanity which seeks fame and popular renown renders a man vulnerable to every breath of popular displeasure, so that there are no such cowards as politicians. He who is quite indifferent to fame will dare all things.

The kingdom, as before, means both the earthly and the mystical kingdom. The safe ruler is he who has freed himself from the slavery of ambitious vanity. He who has trampled self under foot, is ready to be entrusted with the task of governing himself.

The same truth is taught in *Light on the Path*:

"That power which the disciple shall covet is that which shall make him appear as nothing in the eyes of men."[11]

14

You seek the Way, but see it not: it is called colourless.

You listen, but hear it not: it is called soundless.

You would grasp it, but cannot touch it: it is called bodiless.

These three qualities cannot be expressed in words. Therefore they are taken together, and it is called the One.

Its higher part is not manifest; its lower part is not hidden.

It is eternal and cannot be named.

It returns to the unmanifested.

It is called the formless form, the imageless image.

It is called the undefined, the undetermined.

Who meets it, sees not its face; who follows it, sees not its back.

By discerning the immemorial Way, the things of to-day may be governed.

He who understands what was in the beginning, is said to hold the clue of the Way.

Light on the Path again furnishes the best comment:

"Seek out the way. ... Hold fast to that which has neither substance nor existence. Listen only to the voice which is soundless. Look only on that which is invisible alike to the inner and the outer sense."[12]

The higher part of the Way is not yet manifest to us. The small, old path which the seers tread, stretches far away.[13] But its lower part is not hidden. Each one of us, every human being without exception, is even now standing on the road; is at a point from which, if he gives his heart to it, he can go forward on the path of the seers. The duty nearest to hand is the golden opportunity; if rightly done, for the sake of the Way, he has already begun to go forward on the Way. Therefore its lower part is not hidden. Following that Way, the soul returns to the home from which it set out so long ago. What was in the beginning, is the soul. He who begins to obey the soul, holds the clue that will guide him on the Way.

The formless form, the imageless image, indicate the Way, the Logos, as the Creative Power; storehouse of the prototypes, the ideas, in Plato's sense, of all forms and images to be created. We may get an apt illustration in the germ plasm before embryonic development begins: no form is visible, yet the form is there; no image can be perceived, yet the image will in due time completely manifest itself. Paul's sentence, already quoted, expresses exactly the same truth.[14]

15

Those of old, the Masters of the Way, were detached and subtle.

So deep were they, that men knew them not.

Since they could not be observed, I shall endeavour to indicate what they were.

They were circumspect as he who crosses a torrent in winter.

They were alert as he who fears those about him.

They were reserved as a guest.

They were self-effacing as melting ice.
They were natural as uncarved wood.
They were lowly as a valley.
They were impenetrable as troubled water.
Who can make the troubled clear? By stillness it will become clear.
Who can bring life to birth? In quietude it will come to birth.
Who follows the Way seeks not to be overfilled.
Since he is not full of self, he recognises his faults and seeks not to be judged
   perfect.

Perhaps the quaintest expression of the seclusion of the Masters of wisdom is that in
the *Bhagavad Gita*:

"At the end of many births, the possessor of wisdom comes to Me, perceiving that
the Logos is the All; such a one of mighty soul (Mahatma) is very hard to find."[15]

The same truth is set forth, with the reason for it, in *Light on the Path*:

"There are certain spots on the earth where the advance of 'civilization' is unfelt,
and the nineteenth century fever is kept at bay. In these favoured places there is
always time, always opportunity, for the realities of life; they are not crowded out
by the doings of an inchoate, money-loving, pleasure-seeking society. While there
are adepts upon the earth, the earth must preserve to them places of seclusion. This
is a fact in nature which is only an expression of a profound fact in super-nature. . . .
The same state exists in the super-astral life; and the adept has an even deeper and
more profound seclusion there in which to dwell. . . . He is, in his own person, a
treasure of the universal nature, which is guarded and made safe in order that the
fruition shall be perfected."[16]

Therefore the Masters of the Way are so deep that men know them not. They are lowly
as the valley. Therefore one of them has said: "I am the Way. . . . I am meek and lowly in
heart."[17]

But, though hidden, the Masters of the Way may be found; once more to quote the
Bhagavad Gita:

"Sounding the syllable Om, for the Eternal, with heart set upon Me, who goes
forth thus, putting off the body, he enters on the highest Way. He who ever rests
his heart on Me, with no other thought, for him I am easy to find."[18]

And once again, *Light on the Path*:

"For those who are strong enough to conquer the vices of the personal human
nature, the adept is consciously at hand, easily recognized, ready to answer."[19]

So Lao Tzu says that the Masters of the Way are impenetrable as troubled water. Who
can make the troubled clear? By stillness it will become clear. Who can bring life to birth?
In quietude it will come to birth. This again is exactly the thought of the *Bhagavad Gita*:

"Where thought enters the silence, stilled by the practice of union, there, verily,
through the soul beholding the Soul, he finds joy in the Soul."[20]

Lao Tzu continues to develop the same thought.

16

Seek emptiness of self. Seek stillness.
All things manifest themselves and then return.
When the plant has blossomed, it returns to the root.
The return to the root is called stillness.
That stillness may be called a reporting that it has fulfilled its task.
This reporting of fulfilment is the immemorial rule. To know the immemorial
    rule, is to be wise.
To ignore it, leads to impetuous and evil motions.
To know the immemorial rule, brings power and forbearance.
Power and forbearance bring compassion.
Compassion brings a kingly heart.
He who is kinglike, grows heavenlike.
Through likeness to Heaven, he possesses the Way.
Possessing the Way, he is eternal; his powers will never fail.

In the autumn, the rose loses blossoms and leaves. The life-power withdraws to the
root, and the plant becomes dormant, as it was in the early spring. But the summer's
growth has added to the rose, a new store is gathered in.

So is it with the soul. Coming forth from the Eternal, it turns again and takes the Way
homeward to the Eternal, enriched by the harvest of life; thereby enriching the Eternal.

Katha Upanishad puts this well:

"The Self-Being pierced the openings outward; hence one looks outward, not
within himself. A wise man looked toward the Self with reverted sight, seeking
immortality."[21]

But it is possible to turn towards the Self, only by turning away from self. This
renunciation and denial of all the wills of self brings sovereign virtues: power,
forbearance, compassion, the kingly heart, likeness to the Way, the Logos.

Of the kingly heart, a Chinese commentator says:

"He who empties his heart of self, can contain and embrace therein all beings. He
who can contain and suffer all beings, has immeasurable equity and justice; he is
free from partiality. To be just, equitable and impartial is the kingly Way. As the
Way of Heaven is perfectly righteous, the Way of the king, being perfectly
righteous, is the Way of Heaven. The Way nourishes all beings; the king imitates
this Way. He who possesses the Way, extends his benefit over all beings, over all
creatures."

The king, as before, is both the Master, ruler of "the kingdom of heaven", and the
earthly king, for whom the heavenly king is the model and ideal.

17

In the highest degree, men know only that they have rulers.
In the second degree, they love and praise their rulers.
In the third degree, they fear them.

In the fourth degree, they despise them.
When the rulers lose faith in the Way, the people lose faith in their rulers.
The first rulers are guarded and reticent. While they fulfil their task and
   complete their work, the people say: We follow our nature.

It would seem that the first four sentences may mean either four degrees of excellence,
or the four traditional ages: of gold, silver, bronze and iron; in the last of which we are.

But the meaning is exactly the same. The kings of the golden age were kings of the
highest degree; the King-Initiates of tradition, who led each man along the path of his own
soul, inwardly co-operating with the soul. The will of the Higher Self and the will of the
Master are one.

Rulers of the second degree, no longer ministering inwardly to the soul, seek to gain
admiration through gifts and benefits. And so through the four degrees. Exactly the same
thing might be said of churches, or of men, or of women.

18

When the Way was no longer followed,
   humanity and justice were remarked.
When wisdom and prudence came into sight,
   great deceit showed itself.
When harmony no longer governed the six kinships,
   the bonds of family love grew conspicuous.
When states fell into disorder, loyalty and devotion were noted.

Lao Tzu recurs to the idea already touched on: Difficult and easy define each other; long
and short reveal each other; former and latter define each other. In the earliest sinless races,
the thought of holiness could not arise, as in broad daylight no one uses a candle.

But true holiness is a willed turning from sin; true sacrifice is the giving up of a
cherished self-will.

Therefore the present age has its advantage. There can be a willed seeking of the Light,
a willingly rendered obedience. Therefore it has been said that more spiritual progress can
be made in the iron age than in the golden. But a better golden age lies ahead.

19

When wisdom and prudence are no longer noteworthy,
   the people will be happier a hundredfold.
When humanity and justice cease to be noted,
   the people will be once more kindly and filial.
When craft is forgotten and gain undesired,
   thieves and robbers will disappear.
Renounce these three, and know that seeming renunciation is
   not enough.
Therefore I show men what they should seek:
To show simplicity, keep purity, renounce selfishness, abandon desires.

This way of return to the golden age is, in fact, the way of the disciple; through the renunciation of all the wills of self, with their accumulated sins, to return to the simplicity of obedience; to find joy in the eager effort of obedience instead of in the satisfaction of desire; once more to follow the Way of the Eternal, and thereby to inherit the divine blessedness of the Way, the riches of the Logos.

20

Give up the desire to be more learned than others, and you will be freed from care.
How small is the difference between the obedient "yes!" and the disobedient "yea!"
How great is the difference between good and evil.
What all men fear, is easily feared.
They fall into confusion, not checking themselves.
They are carried away, like one who feasts, or one mounted on a tower in spring.
I alone am still; my desires are not aroused.
I am as a new-born child that has not yet smiled to its mother.
I am detached; I seem to have no home.
The multitude have many possessions; I am as one who has lost all.
My thought is indrawn; I seem to know nothing.
The world is wise and prudent; I seem plunged in darkness.
The world is keen; I seem as one bewildered.
I am as a shoreless sea; a barque without a port.
The world is impetuous; I seem inert, like a rustic.
I am apart from other men, because I worship the all-nourishing Mother, the Way.

Lao Tzu contrasts the show of outer learning with the pursuit of inner wisdom. Both consist in learning; therefore they are alike, as are "yes" and "yea", yet difference of motive makes them as unlike as good and evil.

This introduces other contrasts between the way of the world and the Way of the disciple. The world is carried outward by desire; the disciple seeks the inward home. The world is headlong. The disciple enters the silence, detached as a new-born child.

The contrast runs through all writings that speak of the soul. We may find a parallel in Saint Francis:

"As pilgrims and strangers in this world, serving the Lord in poverty and humility, let them go confidently in search of alms. This, my dearest brothers, is the height of the most sublime poverty which has made you heirs and kings of the kingdom of heaven: poor in goods, but exalted in virtue. Let that be your portion, for it leads to the land of the living."[22]

Or we may find our illustration in Isaiah:

"For he shall grow up before him as a tender plant, and as a root out of a dry ground: he hath no form nor comeliness; and when we shall see him, there is no beauty that we should desire him."[23]

Equally apposite would be a passage from the *Katha Upanishad*:

"Thou indeed, pondering on dear and dearly-loved desires, hast passed them by.

Not this way of wealth hast thou chosen, in which many men sink. . . ."[24]

For all are equally concerned with the destruction of the fortresses of self, that we may begin to build the house not made with hands, eternal in the heavens.

Concerning this task, one might quote the whole of *Light on the Path*. A part of one passage must suffice:

"When the disciple has fully recognized that the very thought of individual rights is only the outcome of the venomous quality in himself, that it is the hiss of the snake of self which poisons with its sting his own life and the lives of those about him, then he is ready to take part in a yearly ceremony which is open to all neophytes who are prepared for it. All weapons of defence and offence are given up; all weapons of mind and heart and brain and spirit. . . . From that ceremony he returns into the world as helpless, as unprotected, as a new-born child. . . ."[25]

Therefore Lao Tzu says: I am as one who has lost all; I seem as one bewildered, a barque without a port.

21

The visible forms of the Great Virtue emanate solely from the Way.
This is the nature of the Way:
It is without form, It is concealed.
How formless It is, how well concealed!
Within It are the forms of beings.
How well concealed It is, how formless!
Within It are beings.
How profound It is, how deeply hidden!
Within It is the Spiritual Power. This Spiritual Power is enduring and true.
Within It is the unchanging Witness; from of old until now,
    Its name remains.
It is the door through which all beings come forth.
How do I know that it is thus with all beings?
    I know it through the Way.

If, following the early translators, we were to write Logos in this passage, to express the Chinese word, Tao, it would be at once quite easily understood. Taking the Great Virtue to be the feminine, the form aspect of the Logos, in Sanskrit the feminine Viraj, the primordial Prakriti,[26] "The Soul of matter, the passive female principle from which everything in this Universe emanated,"[27] the masculine aspect of the Logos is spiritual force, which sends forms forth into manifestation.

We can see exactly the same process in our minds, which are small copies of the Logos. In our minds are the images of what we have perceived. The will, the masculine principle, selects its material from these forms and creates some definite mind-image, some picture in the imagination. For example, Shakespeare, gathering many impressions from men and women, used the creative will to form Hamlet and Portia. The actor or actress, using the same creative imagination, takes Shakespeare's words and makes Hamlet and Portia visible.

This understanding of Tao as the Logos is completely in harmony with the great Chinese commentaries, one of which says: "Beginning with the heavens and the earth, down to the myriad beings, all things that have a body, a form, all things that can be seen, are the visible forms of the Great Virtue. They all come forth from Tao." And again: "Tao is bodiless. When It moves through the universe, It becomes the Great Virtue, and then It takes form. This is why the Great Virtue is the manifestation of Tao. Therefore it may be understood that all perceptible forms are the manifestation of Tao in creatures. . . . Tao has neither body nor visible form. Yet, although called bodiless, It contains all beings." To which another commentary adds: "It furnishes the substance of all beings." And, commenting on later words of this passage, the authority first cited says: "All beings without exception pass away. Tao alone passes not away."

This is thoroughly in harmony with all the teachings of the Eastern Wisdom, as set forth, for example, in the Upanishads.

22

The partial becomes complete.
The crooked becomes straight.
The empty becomes full.
The worn out becomes new.
He who has little (desire) finds the Way; he who has much, goes astray.
Therefore the Master keeps the oneness of the Way; he is the model of the world.
He seeks not to be seen, therefore he gives light.
He does not magnify himself, therefore he gives inspiration.
He does not vaunt himself, therefore he has true worth.
He does not glorify himself, therefore he is above all.
He strives not, therefore none in the kingdom can stand against him.
The saying of the ancients: "The partial becomes complete," is not an empty
  phrase.
When a man has attained, the whole world is subject to him.

It has often been said that this ancient Chinese book, written between five and six hundred years before the birth of Christ, is peculiarly Christian in feeling, as, for example, in the emphasis laid on humility. The passage rendered above, well illustrates this.

We might take, for example, the text which the Master Christ took for his first public teaching in the synagogue of his own city, Nazareth, shortly after the temptation in the wilderness:

"And he came to Nazareth, where he had been brought up: and, as his custom was, he went into the synagogue on the sabbath day, and stood up for to read. And there was delivered unto him the book of the prophet Esaias. And when he had opened the book, he found the place where it was written, The Spirit of the Lord is upon me, because he hath anointed me to preach the gospel to the poor; he hath sent me to heal the brokenhearted, to preach deliverance to the captives, and recovery of sight to the blind, to set at liberty them that are bruised, to preach the acceptable year of the Lord. And he closed the book, and he gave it again to the minister, and sat down. And the eyes of all them that were in the synagogue were fastened on him. And he began to say unto them, This day is this Scripture fulfilled in your ears. And all bare him witness, and wondered at the gracious words which proceeded out of his mouth."[28]

For it is the work of the holy and healing Logos, as of the Master who declares himself to be the Way, to fill the empty, to make the crooked straight, to give new life to the worn and heavy laden.

And one may quote, perhaps, in supplement, his later words, recorded by the beloved disciple:

"Because thou sayest, I am rich, and increased with goods, and have need of nothing: and knowest not that thou art wretched, and miserable, and poor, and blind, and naked: I counsel thee to buy of me gold tried in the fire, that thou mayest be rich; and white raiment, that thou mayest be clothed, and that the shame of thy nakedness do not appear; and anoint thine eyes with eyesalve, that thou mayest see. As many as I love, I rebuke and chasten: be zealous therefore, and repent."[29]

Perhaps a closer translation of the last verse would be: "As many as I love, I convince and train as children; be zealous therefore, and change thy heart."

The divine Logos, the Master who is the manifested life of the Logos, remains hidden, seeking not to glorify himself; he gives spiritual light and inspiration, making the blind see, healing the brokenhearted. He is unseen, yet the whole world is subject to him, as King.

23

He who keeps silence, gains detachment.
The tempest does not endure all the morning; the rain storm does not last all day.
What produces these two? Heaven and earth produce them.
If heaven and earth cannot maintain (tempestuous violence), how then can man?
Therefore, the man who gives himself to the Way, becomes one with the Way;
    he who gives himself to righteousness, becomes one with righteousness;
    he who gives himself to evil, becomes one with evil.
He who becomes one with the Way, gains the Way;
    he who becomes one with righteousness, gains righteousness;
    he who becomes one with evil, gains (the shame of) evil.
He who does not give all (for the Way), ends by losing the Way.

Regarding the opening phrase, a Chinese commentator humorously says:

"The immoderate love of discussion comes from an interior disturbance of the soul, just as the tempest and the rain storm are produced by the disordered action of heaven and earth. If, then, the disturbance of heaven and earth cannot long endure, it will be the same thing, in even greater degree, with the talkativeness of man."

The same commentator further says:

"He who has true self-confidence, gains the trust of the men of his time, even when he is silent. But those who love discussion, who ceaselessly abandon themselves to the intemperance of the tongue, the more they speak, the less they are believed. This distrust comes wholly from the fact that they have no true self-confidence."

24

Who raises himself on tiptoe, stands not firm;
  who strains his stride, walks not far.
Who contends for his own view, finds not wisdom.
Who is self-complacent, gives no light.
Who boasts of himself, has no true worth.
Who glorifies himself, shall not long endure.
Viewed from the Way, these acts are like the leavings of a feast,
  like a repulsive tumour.
Therefore, he who has found the Way, shuns these things.

A Chinese commentator says:

"He who stands on tiptoe seeks only to raise his head above others, forgetting that he cannot keep this posture. He who strains his stride, seeks only to outstrip others, forgetting that he cannot continue."

Another commentary says:

"He who is self-complacent, with a sort of partiality for himself, imagines that all other men have less wit than he; he cannot profit by their gifts, therefore he finds not wisdom."

Which would seem to be the Chinese expression of the Theosophical method.

Yet another commentator says:

"He who has found the Way, perseveres in humility."

25

There is unmanifested Being, which existed before the heavens and the earth.
How still It is, and bodiless!
It stands alone, unchanging.
It moves through all things, unmenaced.
It may be regarded as the Mother of the universe.
Its name I know not.
To give It a name, I call It the Way.
To describe It, I call It Great.
Being Great, I call It elusive.
Being elusive, I call It far-reaching.
Being far-reaching, I say It returns.
This is why the Way is great, the heavens are great, the earth is great,
  the King is great.
Man follows the earth; earth follows heaven; heaven follows the Way; the Way
  follows Its own Being.

One of the commentators says:

"If I am asked concerning this Being (the Way), I answer: It has neither head nor tail; It is neither modified nor changed; It has no body or determined place; It knows neither over-abundance nor lack, neither diminution nor increase; It wanes not; It is not born; It is neither yellow nor red, neither white nor blue; It has neither inside nor outside, neither sound nor smell, neither depth nor height, neither form nor brilliance."

This is exactly the method followed in the Upanishads: defining the Eternal by the negatives of everything that is not the Eternal, "Unborn, undying, unindicable."

Another Chinese commentator says:

"The Way has no companion in the universe. It dwells outside the limits of beings, and has never changed. Upward, it rises to the heavens; downward, it penetrates to the abysses. It circulates throughout the universe and can suffer no detriment."

Other commentaries add:

"The sun's heat burns It not; dampness rots It not; It passes through all bodies and incurs no danger. It expands throughout the heavens and the earth, and dwells in the hearts of all beings; It is the source of all births, the root of all transformations. The heavens, the earth, man and all creatures, have need of It, that they may live. It nourishes all beings as a mother nourishes her children. This is why Lao Tzu says, It may be regarded as the Mother of the universe."

26

Heavy is the root of light; stillness, the master of motion.
Therefore the sage walks ever in the Way, keeping stillness and poise.
Though he possess splendid palaces, he remains detached and still.
Yet the lord of ten thousand chariots may act lightly in his kingdom.
Through lightness he loses his ministers; following desire, he forfeits his throne.

The Chinese commentators say

"Lao Tzu wishes men to master their passions through stillness and poise. He who is inwardly poised, is exempt from the levity of the passions; he whose heart is still, cannot be carried away by anger. He who can control himself, is poised; he who keeps his place, is still. The man with poise subdues the man of levity; he who is still, subdues him who is carried away."

For the last two sentences of the text, we may cite Emerson's phrase:

"We forfeit the thrones of angels for temporary pleasures."[30]

27

Who walks wisely, leaves no footprints;
  who speaks wisely, makes no mistakes;

who reckons wisely, uses no tally;
who closes wisely, needs no lock, nor can it be opened;
who binds wisely, needs no cord, nor can it be loosed.
Therefore the Master, working justly, seeks to save all, rejecting none.
Working with justice, he seeks to save all; this is why he rejects none.
He has light, and again light.
Therefore the righteous is master of the unrighteous.
The unrighteous is the opportunity of the righteous.
If the one regard not his master, if the other love not his opportunity, though
    they be prudent, both are blind.
This is the great mystery.

A Chinese commentary says:

"He who follows the Way, walks without need of feet, speaks without opening his
lips, determines wisely without the measuring of the mind; what he has closed
cannot be opened; what he has bound cannot be loosed; for he imprisons his
passions and chains his desires."

Considering later sentences of the text, another commentary says:

"Those whom the world calls wise, follow narrow ways. They give with partiality,
and know not that justice which is broad and liberal toward all. Whom they
esteem virtuous, and like themselves, they are ready to save. But him who seems not
virtuous, they hate and cannot love. Therefore they reject many men and many
beings. But the holy man is free from partiality, and instructs all without
preference. He seeks to save all men and all beings; therefore, there is no man, nor
any being, whom he rejects. The holy man is not holy for himself alone; he is
destined to be the exemplar of all men. If those who have no virtue will follow his
leading, they may be rid of their faults and attain virtue. Therefore he who has
virtue is master of those who have not virtue."

28

Who knows his strength, yet retains gentleness, is the valley of the kingdom.
    (All flows to him.)
If he be the valley of the kingdom, humility abides with him; he becomes again
    a little child.
Who knows his light, yet retains darkness, is the exemplar of the kingdom.
If he be the exemplar of the kingdom, holiness abides with him; he becomes
    again perfect.
Who knows his glory, yet retains humility, is likewise the valley of the kingdom.
If he be the valley of the kingdom, his righteousness is made perfect; he gains
    again the perfect simplicity (of the Way).
When the perfect simplicity (of the Way) is spread abroad, it moulds all beings.
When the holy man attains, he becomes the ruler in the kingdom. Governing
    all, he injures none.

This is once more the teaching of humility, the spirit of the valley, which permeates and inspires the whole book. When the simplicity of the Way, the light of the Logos, the spirit of the Master, shall be received into all hearts, it will mould all beings according to the spirit of the Way. This is the coming of the kingdom.

29

Who seeks to remake the kingdom, will certainly fail.
The kingdom is divinely planned; man cannot remake it.
If he seek to remake, he destroys; if he seek to seize, he loses.
Among beings, some go before, some follow;
    some are hot, some are cold;
    some are strong, some are weak;
    some move, others halt.
Therefore the sage refrains from excess, luxury, indulgence.

Lao Tzu has, in the first three sentences, a striking epigram, a general statement of nearly all of human life, whether of the individual or of multitudes. For what are most men and most movements doing, if not seeking "to remake the kingdom of heaven" according to their own desires? But the kingdom is divinely ordained of old; its perpetual laws are to be sought and obeyed. Our amendments will not be carried.

The fourth sentence seems to reinforce this thought by a parable. Men and things are what they are: some are swift, others are slow; some are hot, others are cold. Just as we cannot make men and things over, but must accept them, so we cannot make over the kingdom of heaven.

Therefore the sage, discerning the laws of the kingdom and accepting them, conquers that in him which rebels against the kingdom, and refrains from excess and self-indulgence.

30

He who works for the Master of men in accordance with the Way, seeks not to
    advance the kingdom by compulsion.
For men render again what they receive.
Where armies halt, spring up thorns and briars.
In the wake of wars come years of fasting.
The sage strikes resolutely and remains still. He dares not advance the kingdom
    by compulsion.
He strikes resolutely, without vaunting himself.
He strikes resolutely, without boasting.
He strikes resolutely, without arrogance.
He strikes resolutely, but only when a blow must be struck.
He strikes resolutely, but without self-assertion.
The things of nature ripen; then they fade.
Not so is it with the Way. Who follows not the Way, comes to destruction.

If the preceding sentences were an epigram on men and their desires, then the present sentences are a criticism of nearly all ecclesiastical history; of all those, esteeming themselves to be the only righteous, who seek "to advance the kingdom by compulsion." Where they have passed, spring thorns and briars, as in the wake of an army. After their wars, comes spiritual starvation.

The Master seeks to win, not to tyrannize and compel. Having the power to force compliance, he draws, instead, with the cords of love.

31

Weapons of offence, however keen, work evil:
All men hate them. Therefore he who has found the Way is unwilling to use
    them.
In peace, the sage esteems the left; he who makes war esteems the right.
Weapons of offence work evil; these are not the weapons of the sage.
He uses them from necessity only, but esteems stillness and quietude.
In victory he is not elated. To be elated is to love destruction.
He who loves destruction cannot rule over the kingdom.
In times of rejoicing the left is preferred;
    in times of mourning the right is preferred.
The second in command occupies the left;
    the commander in chief occupies the right.
I mean that he takes the place of mourning.
He who has slain a multitude of men should weep over them with tears and sobs.
The victor in the battle takes the place of mourning.

We have the choice of two interpretations for this section of the Chinese sage's book. We may take what is said above simply in the sense of that pacifism which has saturated the people of the Middle Kingdom for the last seven centuries, leaving them, as a nation, at the mercy of foreign conquerors, beginning with the virile race of Genghis Khan, "Khan of Khans," Prince of Princes, the greatest military family in the history of Asia. It is in the sense of pacifism that the Chinese commentators, for the most part, interpret these sections; for example:

"The sage thinks constantly of peace, of non-action, and abstains from war. He who believes that the better plan is not to wage war shows that he holds precious the lives of men."

But there is a deeper and more mystical sense in which we may understand what Lao Tzu has written, that, namely, which is set forth in the fourth Comment in *Light on the Path:*

"When the disciple has fully recognized that the very thought of individual rights is only the outcome of the venomous quality in himself, that it is the hiss of the snake of self which poisons with its sting his own life and the lives of those about him, then he is ready to take part in a yearly ceremony which is open to all neophytes who are prepared for it. All weapons of defence and offence are given up;

all weapons of mind and heart, and brain, and spirit. Never again can another man be regarded as a person who can be criticized or condemned; never again can the neophyte raise his voice in self-defence or excuse. From that ceremony he returns into the world as helpless, as unprotected, as a new-born child. That, indeed, is what he is. He has begun to be born again on the higher plane of life, that breezy and well-lit plateau from whence the eyes see intelligently and regard the world with a new insight."[31]

This stage in the spiritual life of the disciple would appear to be the theme of Isaiah, when he writes: "He is despised and rejected of men; a man of sorrows, and acquainted with grief: . . . He was oppressed, and he was afflicted, yet he opened not his mouth: he is brought as a lamb to the slaughter, and as a sheep before her shearers is dumb, so he openeth not his mouth. . . . He shall see of the travail of his soul, and shall be satisfied: by his knowledge shall my righteous servant justify many; for he shall bear their iniquities. Therefore will I divide him a portion with the great, and he shall divide the spoil with the strong; because he hath poured out his soul unto death."[32]

And the same thing is true of those passages in the Sermon on the Mount, on which is based the doctrine of non-resistance.[33] The Greek word really means to "set evil against evil";[34] the disciple is warned against this, exactly as in *Light on the Path*. But there is an abyss of difference between the refusal to return hate for hate and the failure, whether from weakness or cowardice, to protect others. The mistaken application of this spiritual principle has made China helpless for centuries.

There remains the curious passage regarding the positions of left and right. Concerning this, a Chinese commentator says that the left side corresponds to the active principle; it is the symbol of life: therefore in ceremonies of happiness, the left is preferred. The right side corresponds to the inert principle; it is the symbol of death; therefore in ceremonies of mourning, the right is preferred.

Perhaps the left side is preferred as being "nearest the heart"; but we need not look for a deep principle here any more than we need look for an Occult reason why "Keep to the left" is the rule of the road in England, while other nations keep to the right.

32

The Way, as the Eternal, has no name.

Though according to Its nature It is without size, the whole world could not overcome It.

When princes and kings follow It, all beings submit themselves to them.

Then will Heaven and Earth unite to send down a sweet dew, and the peoples will enter peace without being commanded.

When the Way became differentiated, It took a name.

When this name is established, men must learn to become stable.

He who is stable is free from peril.

The Way extends throughout the universe.

As the streams and torrents of the mountains return to the rivers and the seas (so all beings return to the Way).

A Chinese commentator says that Heaven and Earth, men and all beings, draw their origin from the Way. This is why they can influence each other, establishing correspondences between them. If princes and kings can truly keep to the Way, all beings will come to submit themselves to them; Heaven and Earth will of themselves enter into harmony, and the hundred families will attain to peace.

The Way, says another native commentator, is of its own nature invisible and immaterial. At the time when beings had not been manifested, no name could be given to It. But when Its divine influence had wrought transformations, and when beings had come forth from the unmanifest, It received Its name from beings. As soon as Heaven and Earth had become manifest, all beings were born from the Way; this is why It is regarded as the Mother of all beings.

To be stable, says another commentator, is to stand, not allured and drawn away by the things of sense, but resting in perfect quietude, self-poised; then one is free from all danger.

Heaven and Earth are used here, exactly as in the Upanishads, and, indeed, universally in the primeval tradition which survives from the islands of the Pacific to Mexico,[35] for the positive and negative aspects of the manifested Logos, called in the Sankhya philosophy, Purusha and Prakriti, Spirit and Nature.[36]

A commentator says that all rivers and seas are the place where the waters unite; the streams and torrents of the mountains are parts and subdivisions of the waters. The Way is the source of all beings; all beings are branchings of the Way. All the streams and torrents of the mountains return to the central gathering place of the waters, and in the same way all beings return to their place of origin, the Way, from which they set out.

Exactly the same image is used in many Upanishads, as, for example:

"And as these rivers, rolling oceanwards, go to their setting on reaching the ocean, and their name and form are lost in the ocean, so the sixteen parts of this seer, moving spiritwards, on reaching Spirit, go to their setting; their name and form are lost in Spirit. This seer becomes one, without parts, immortal."[37]

There is a kindred passage, "By command of this Eternal, rivers roll eastward and westward from the white mountains", in the *Brihad Aranyaka Upanishad*.[38]

33

He who knows other men is prudent.
He who knows himself is wise.
He who rules other men is potent.
He who rules himself is strong.
He who suffices to himself is rich.
He who acts with energy is possessed of a strong will.
He who departs not from his own nature endures long.
He who dies and yet endures has everlasting life.

He who knows other men, says a Chinese commentator, is prudent; he sees external things. His knowledge is limited to knowing the good and bad qualities of men, the superiority or inferiority of their talents.

He who knows himself is illuminated; he is endowed with the inner sight. He alone can know himself who concentrates within himself his hearing, to hear That which has no sound, and his vision, to see That which has no body.

Here again *Light on the Path* may be quoted:

"Listen only to the voice which is soundless. Look only on that which is invisible alike to the inner and the outer sense."[39]

Another commentator says that he who suffices not to himself has insatiate desires; even if he had abounding riches, he would be as one in want. Such a man cannot call himself rich. He alone deserves the name, who suffices to himself, who remains calm and free from desire.

Commenting on the sentences which follow, a Chinese writer says:

"He who cannot act with energy, to reach the Way, often fails in his designs. His will is not firm. But the sage who acts with energy, ever advances in the Way; the farther off the Way appears, the more his will is enkindled to seek It."

The comment of a native writer on the last phrase of the text is full of interest. He says that "Lao Tzu's words, 'dies and yet endures', Chwang Tse's expression, 'not to die,' and the Buddhist 'not to be extinguished', have exactly the same meaning. The body of man is exactly like the case of a chrysalis or the slough of a serpent. Now, when the case of the chrysalis is left dried up, the insect is not dead; when the serpent's slough rots, the serpent is not dead." And another commentator adds: "The animal life of man is dissipated, but the soul remains for ever."

One may compare the simile in the Upanishad:

"And like as the slough of a snake lies lifeless, cast forth upon an ant-hill, so lies his body, when the Spirit of man rises up bodiless and immortal, as the Life, as the Eternal, as the Radiance."[40]

The secret is that continual dying to self and to the world, for love of the Eternal, which Saint Paul had in mind when he said, "I die daily",[41] a phrase that had been used earlier by Philo.

"The sage", says another Chinese writer, "looks on life and death as the morning and the evening. He exists, but is detached from life; he dies, yet endures. This is what is called life everlasting."

He is "the true alchemist, in possession of the elixir of life."[42]

34

The Way stretches everywhere; It can go to the left as well as to the right.
All beings rely on It for their life, and It fails them not.
When Its works are accomplished, It does not attribute them to Itself.
It loves and nourishes all beings, but does not seek to constrain them.
Ever free from desires, It may be called little.
All beings are subject to It, It constrains them not. It may be called great.
Therefore, to the end of his life, the holy man does not regard himself as great.
This is why he can accomplish great things.

The Way, says a commentator, flows everywhere, through the heavens and the earth, and the hearts of the myriad beings; It is on the right, It is on the left; It has neither body nor name.

Another commentator says that, in the beginning, the Way gave life to all beings, and, at the end, It leads them to their perfect fruition. In the most perfect way, It loves and nourishes all beings in the universe. Nevertheless, though it heap all beings with blessings, It never seeks to constrain them, to force their wills, to destroy their spiritual liberty.

35

The holy man preserves the great Principle (the Way), and all the peoples of the
    kingdom hasten to him.
They run together, and he does them no injury; he brings them peace and calm
    and quietude.
Music and banquets hold the passing traveller.
But when the Way comes forth from our lips, it is flat and tasteless.
It is looked for and cannot be seen; It is listened for and cannot be heard; It is
    used and cannot be exhausted.

When the music ceases, say the commentators, when the banquet comes to an end, the traveller hastily withdraws. This comparison shows that the joys of this world are fleeting and illusive. Not so with the Way. Though It does not delight the ears nor flatter the palate, like music and banquets, yet, when It is followed and applied to life, It can pervade the whole world and endure through the generations.

36

That which contracts has surely expanded.
That which grows weak has surely been strong.
That which fades has surely been bright.
That which grows poor has surely been endowed with gifts.
This is both hidden and revealed.
The gentle triumphs over the hard; the weak triumphs over the strong.
The fish should not leave the depths; the strong arm of the kingdom should not
    be shown to the people.

The sense seems to be exactly that of the proverb, "What goes up must come down." It is a contrast between the world of the Eternal and the external world of the "pairs of opposites", where all things change and endure not; where moth and rust doth corrupt, and where thieves break through and steal.

As to what follows, it is, say the commentators, a doctrine hidden from the foolish, but revealed to the wise. The Way, which is gentle, triumphs over that which is hard; the Way, which seems weak, triumphs over the strong.

Then comes a quaint conceit of Celestial humour:

"While it is in the soft element, water, the fish is safe; on the hard element, earth, it comes to grief. In the same way, the Master governs without the display of external force."

37

The Way follows non-action, yet accomplishes all things.

If kings and princes follow the Way, all beings will turn to righteousness.

If, after they have turned, they wish again to go astray, I shall hold them back
through that simple Being which is without name.

The simple Being which has no name should not even be desired.

The absence of desire brings peace.

Then the kingdom becomes righteous of itself.

As was earlier pointed out, this Chinese teaching of non-action *(wu wei)* is exactly the
doctrine of the *Bhagavad Gita*:

"Who works, putting all works on the Eternal, giving up attachment, is not
stained by sin, as the lotus leaf by water. . . . He who is united, giving up the fruit of
works, wins perfect peace; the ununited, attached to the fruit of his works, is bound
by the force of his desire."[43]

The Chinese commentator works the matter out methodically. Long after the people
have turned toward righteousness, he says, affections and desires will begin to stir again in
the bottom of their hearts, and virtue will wane. But the holy man in good time perceives
this grave defect and checks it in its first beginnings. With the help of that which is simple
and unnamed, the Way of the Spirit, and through detachment, he checks the first stirrings
of passion. But if one should seek the Way with desire, this is still desire; therefore the Way
must not be sought with desire. When the Way is no longer sought with desire, perfect
quietude of heart is attained, and when desire has ceased in the heart, righteousness comes of
itself. When freedom from desire has spread throughout the kingdom, the kingdom
becomes righteous of itself.

Or, to give the same thought a Western turn: We must seek God for God's own sake, not
for His gifts.

Or we may cite the words attributed to a Master: "Is there none who will serve me
gratis?"

38

Those who have the highest righteousness do not consider that they are
righteous; therefore they are righteous.

Those of lesser righteousness never forget that they are righteous; this is why
they are not truly righteous.

Those who have the highest righteousness act righteously without thinking of
righteousness.

The men of lesser righteousness are consciously righteous.

Those who have supreme humanity act rightly without thinking of humanity.

Those who weigh human rights practise them self-consciously.

Those who follow formalism practise it, and the people do not respond; then
they use force to make formalism effective.

This is why men become self-consciously righteous after they have lost the Way;

they become self-consciously humane after they have lost righteousness; they concern themselves with the rights of man after they have ceased to be humane; they become formalists after they have lost the sense of the rights of man.

Formalism is only the outer bark of uprightness and sincerity; it is the beginning of disorder.

False wisdom is but the barren flower of the Way and the principle of ignorance.

Therefore the great man cleaves to the substance and ignores mere surfaces.

He honours the fruit and leaves the barren flower.

Therefore he takes the one and rejects the other.

We have here a descending scale: The Way (Tao); self-conscious righteousness; what we may call humanitarianism; concern over the rights of man; and a lifeless formalism. But, at the distance of twenty-five centuries, it is not easy to catch the exact shades of Lao Tzu's meaning.

To begin with the first sentence: "Those who have the highest righteousness do not consider that they are righteous": we may cite, as a parallel: "Except your righteousness shall exceed the righteousness of the scribes and Pharisees, ye shall in no case enter into the kingdom of heaven";[44] or that other saying, with its fine irony: "Joy shall be in heaven over one sinner that repenteth, more than over ninety and nine just persons which need no repentance."[45] Or we may quote the saying that there is nothing more contemptible than self-conscious heroism.

One of the Chinese commentators has this to say of the closing sentences of this section:

"The holy man penetrates all beings by the aid of a marvellous intuition. The true and the false, good and evil, shine in his vision as in a mirror. Nothing escapes his perspicacity. Common men see nothing but what is before their eyes, and hear nothing but what reaches their ears, and think nothing that is beyond their minds. They walk as blind men in the midst of beings; they use their faculties to gain knowledge, and only by chance do they catch gleams of light. They believe that they understand, and do not see that they are going toward the depth of ignorance. They rejoice when they have won what is lowest and vilest in the world, and they lose sight of what is lofty and sublime. They seek after surfaces and neglect realities; they gather the flower and throw away the fruit. Only the great man rejects the flower for the fruit."

Editors generally mark this as the first section of the second part of the *Tao Te Ching*; and, as the word "te", which we have translated "righteousness", occurs ten times in this section, giving the keynote of the second half of the book, it is thought that the general title means the Book of Tao and of Te; that is, the book, the first half of which is concerned with Tao, the second half with Te.

39

These are the things which have gained Unity.

Heaven is pure because it has gained Unity.

Earth is still because it has gained Unity.

The spirits of men are wise because they have gained Unity.

The valleys are filled because they have gained Unity.

The myriad beings are born because they have gained Unity.

Princes and kings are the standard of the world because they have gained Unity.

Such is the fruit of Unity.

If Heaven lost its purity, it would dissolve.

If Earth lost its stillness, it would crumble.

If the spirits of men lost their wisdom, they would cease to be.

If the valleys were not filled, they would dry up.

If the myriad beings were not born, they would come to nothingness.

If princes and kings grew proud of their high station, and ceased to be standards, they would be overthrown.

Therefore nobles remember their common humanity; men of high station remember the lowliness of their beginning.

Therefore princes and kings call themselves orphans, lowly, meek.

Do they not show by this that they remember their common humanity? And they are right!

This is why, if you take a wagon to pieces, you no longer have a wagon.

The wise man seeks no extrinsic value as precious jade, nor would he be despised as a worthless stone.

The Chinese commentator quoted, says:

"Unity is the Way (the Logos). From the Way, all beings have received that which constitutes their nature. Men see beings and forget the Way. They are content to know that Heaven is pure, that Earth is still, that spirits are endowed with intelligence, that valleys may be filled, that myriad beings are born, that princes and kings are standards for mankind. But they forget that it is from the Way that all these qualities are drawn. The greatness of Heaven and Earth, the nobility of princes and kings, is the Unity which has brought them into being. But what is this Unity? You look for it and cannot see it; you wish to touch it and cannot lay hands on it. It is clear that it is the most subtle thing in the world."

If we remember that "the Kingdom" means also the kingdom of heaven, we may believe that princes and kings mean disciples and their Masters, who are in truth the standards of mankind, full of humility, and, therefore, thinking of themselves as meek and lowly of heart.

The cryptic sentence about the wagon is thus explained by a Chinese commentary:

"With a multitude of materials you make a wagon. Wagon is the collective name of the different materials of which a wagon is made. If you count them one by one, if you take the wagon to pieces, you have nave, wheels, spokes, axle, pole and so on, and if you give these different parts their names, the name wagon disappears; there is no longer a wagon. In the same way, the unity of the people brings the prince or king into being. If you take the people away, the ruler disappears. Therefore princes and kings should be lowly in their honours; they should be simple and humble, like the Way."

40

The return to the unmanifest causes the movement of the Way.
Weakness is the method of the Way.
All things in the world are born from the manifest (Logos);
   the manifest is born from the unmanifest.

One might write a treatise on these three sentences. It is better, perhaps, to suggest certain clues to their meaning.

It is said, for example, that "the whole personality must be dissolved",[46] in order that the real individuality may be born. In this sense, the "return" causes the forward movement.

To carry the same thought to its conclusion, he who would become a Master goes back into the hidden depths of Being, in order that he may later come forth to work.

As commentary on the second sentence, we may take the phrases of Saint Paul: "It is sown in weakness, it is raised in power";[47] "And he said unto me, My grace is sufficient for thee: for my strength is made perfect in weakness";[48] and even the mysterious saying: "For though he was crucified through weakness, yet he liveth by the power of God."[49]

41

When those of the highest order of learning hear the Way declared, they follow
   it with zeal.
When those of the second order of learning have heard the Way declared, they
   now follow it, now lose it.
When those of the lowest order of learning have heard the Way declared, they
   mock at it.
If they did not mock at it, it would not deserve to be called the Way.
Therefore those of old said:
He who has the understanding of the Way, seems hidden in darkness.
He who has gone far along the Way, seems backward.
He who has ascended the Way, seems of low estate.
The man of high virtue is like the valley.
The man of perfect purity is as though despised.
The man of infinite worth seems full of weakness.
The man of true virtue appears inert.
The man who is simple and true seems low and degraded.
It is a square so great that its corners cannot be seen.
   It is a vessel so great that it seems uncompleted.

It is a voice so great that its sound is imperceptible.
It is an image so great that its shape is not perceived.
The Way is hidden, so that none can name it.
It lends its aid and leads all beings to perfection.

A Chinese commentator says:

"Those of the highest order of learning understand both what is hidden and what shines forth in the Way; they penetrate beyond the limits of the body. This is why, as soon as they hear the Way declared, they put their faith in it and follow it with zeal. Those of the second order of learning are on the border between the hidden and that which shines forth; between what is hidden from the senses, and what the senses perceive. They stand between the Way and the material world. Therefore, when they have heard the Way declared, they stand half in faith and half in doubt. This is why they now follow the Way, and now lose it. Those of the lowest order of learning see what shines forth, what is perceived by the senses, but not what is hidden. They remain wrapped in matter. Therefore, when they have heard the Way declared, they mock at it."

Another commentator adds:

"The Way is hidden, deep, inscrutable. Those of the lowest order of learning mock at it because they seek it with their senses and cannot find it. If they could reach it, if they could grasp it in its sublimity with their senses, they would not mock at it; but, becoming accessible to their gross vision, it would lose all its grandeur, and would no longer deserve to be called the Way."

Concerning the dozen axioms quoted from those of old, the commentators say:

"The ordinary man uses craft, boasting of it and thinking himself able. The saint has light, but lets it not shine outwardly, nor does he use craft. The ordinary man boasts and pushes himself forward insatiably. The saint dwells in humility, full of the sense of his own abjection and unworthiness. The ordinary man exalts himself. The saint unites himself in heart to the Way. The ordinary man has a narrow soul, which could not hold an atom. The saint holds in his heart the heavens and the earth. The ordinary man is inwardly full of sins and uncleanness; he decks himself outwardly, to appear pure and spotless. The saint is upright and simple, he is pure and white as snow. His righteousness is untarnished by the dust of the world; therefore he is able to bear shame and suffer ignominy. The ordinary man boasts of his least virtue. He wishes to be paid for each of his good acts. The saint sends forth his righteousness and his benefits over all beings, taking no credit to himself for it. Therefore he appears to lack righteousness."

42

The Way produced the One; the One produced the Two; the Two produced the
    Three; the Three produced all beings.
All beings flee from stillness and seek movement.
An immaterial Breath forms harmony.

Men hate to be orphans, lowly and meek; yet the kings so describe themselves.
Therefore, among beings some are exalted because they abase themselves; others
   are abased because they exalt themselves.
I teach what men teach.
The violent and unbending do not meet a natural death.
I shall take their example as the basis of my teachings.

The meaning of the first sentence would seem to be: The Unmanifest produced the Manifest; the Manifest has two aspects, the masculine and feminine Logos.[50] These two produced the Great Breath of manifestation, thus constituting a triad. The Chinese commentaries are in harmony with this interpretation. The Great Breath is also harmony, because it is the universal law of Karma, which "ordains all things wisely through perpetual ages."

The teaching that "whosoever shall exalt himself shall be abased; and he that shall humble himself shall be exalted,"[51] needs little comment. He who humbles his personal will before the Divine Will, becomes one with that Divine Will and, therefore, invincible; but he who asserts his personal, rebellious will, is brought low by the Divine Will, in order that he may learn humility. The kings are those rulers of the heavenly kingdom who are "meek and lowly in heart,"[52] knowing that the Divine Will is all in all.

The next phrase, "I teach what men teach," has divided the commentators; it may be simply the introduction to the next sentence: "The violent and unbending do not meet a natural death"; their fate teaches the need of humility; this I also teach. This would accord well with the following sentence: "I shall take their example as the basis of my teachings."

43

The softest things in the world overcome the hardest things in the world.
The Unmanifest passes through things impenetrable. From this I know that
   non-action (detachment) is useful.
In the world there are few who know how to teach without words, and to draw
   profit from non-action.

"The Way is bodiless," says a Chinese commentator, "therefore it can penetrate minds and hearts and the multitude of beings."
Another commentary says:

   "He who acts actively may fail and lose the merit which   he seeks; he who acts without acting gains limitless success.   In this way Heaven and Earth act; in this way men and beings spring up."

It is exactly the teaching of the *Bhagavad Gita* concerning detachment.
The same wise Celestial goes on to say:

   "The voice which expresses itself in sounds cannot be heard even for a hundred miles; the Voice, which is soundless penetrates beyond Heaven, and moves the kingdom. The words of men are not understood by other races of men; but at the Word of the Being which speaks not, the two principles, masculine and feminine, send forth their fructifying powers, and Heaven and Earth join to bring forth beings. Now the Way and Righteousness do not act, yet Heaven and Earth give beings their entire development. Heaven and Earth do not speak, but the four seasons follow their courses."

This is not only the substance of the Logos doctrine, but the wording also.

44

Which is nearer to us, our renown or our own being?
Which is dearer, our own being or riches?
Which is the greater misfortune, to gain wealth, or to lose it?
Therefore he who has limitless desires is exposed to limitless misfortunes.
He who lays up rich treasures, inevitably suffers great losses.
He who suffices for himself dreads no dishonour.
He who holds himself in check risks no falls.
Such a one endures.

The commentator says, in his dry way:

"Putting aside questions, this means that our own being is nearer to us than renown, dearer to us than riches; that it is a greater misfortune to gain wealth than to lose it."

Another commentator says:

"He who possesses righteousness knows that the fairest nobility dwells in him, therefore he expects nothing from renown. He knows that the most precious treasure abides in him, and therefore expects nothing from what wealth procures. This is why he can hold himself in check, and does not fall. Since he is exposed neither to dishonour nor to danger, he endures."

This is once again the teaching of the goodly pearl, the hidden treasure,[53] which is the divine life hidden in the heart within.[54]

45

The holy man is nobly perfect, yet he appears full of imperfections; his riches are
    not consumed.
He is nobly filled, yet he appears empty; his riches waste not away.
He is nobly upright, yet he appears faulty.
He is nobly discerning, yet he appears simple.
He is nobly eloquent, yet he appears to stammer.
Movement overcomes cold, but quietness overcomes heat.
    The pure and still become the model of the universe.

"The prince," says the commentator, "who possesses the perfection of the Way and of Righteousness, conceals his glory and hides the praises he receives. The prince who possesses the fullness of the Way and of Righteousness appears empty; that is, he is full of honours, and yet dares not to exalt himself; he is rich, and dares not yield to luxury and indulgence." The prince is the disciple of the "kings."

Concerning the last sentence, a commentator has this to say:

"When a man becomes pure, still, detached, though he seek not to triumph over beings, no being can resist him. Therefore Lao Tzu says that the pure and still become the model of the universe."

46

When the Way ruled the world, the horses were sent to till the fields.
When the Way no longer rules, war horses are bred on the frontier.
There is no greater crime than to yield to desires.
There is no greater ill than not to be self-sufficing.
There is no greater loss than the lust of possessions.
He who is self-sufficing is ever content with his fate.

The commentators tend to take the simile of the horses literally, in a sense inclined toward Chinese pacifism. But Lao Tzu so constantly approaches the thought and even the phrases of the Upanishads, drawing, it would seem, from the same perennial springs which inspired the Upanishads, that we are justified in holding that in this instance also he is speaking not in the spirit of pacifism but in the spirit of the hidden wisdom, using the symbols which are called the Mystery language.

If this be so, then we may compare the sentences concerning the horses with a passage in *Katha Upanishad:*

"Know the Higher Self as the lord of the chariot, and the body as the chariot; know the soul as the charioteer, and the mind and emotional nature as the reins. They say that the powers of perception and action are the horses, and that objective things are the roadways for these."[55]

To apply this directly to our text: When we are under the rule of the Way, the Logos, the powers till the inner fields of our hearts and minds; the inner senses, the inner powers of action, come into activity; but when the Way does not rule, the powers are active only on the frontier, the outer fringe of our natures.

In the phrase, "self-sufficing," it should be remembered that we are speaking of the Higher Self, concerning which one of the Upanishads says:

"This is the mighty Soul unborn, who is consciousness among the life-powers. This is the heaven in the heart within, where dwells the ruler of all, master of all, lord of all. He is lord of all, overlord of beings, shepherd of beings. He is the bridge that holds the worlds apart, lest they should flow together. This is he whom the followers of the Eternal seek to know through their scriptures, sacrifices, gifts and penances, through ceasing from evil toward others. He who knows this becomes a sage. This is the goal in search of which pilgrims go forth on pilgrimages."[56]

We are the pilgrims, pilgrims of eternity, and manifested life is the pilgrimage.

47

Without leaving my house, I know the universe; without looking through my
   window, I discover the ways of Heaven.
The farther one goes afield, the less he learns.
This is why the sage goes whither he will without going abroad;
   he names things without setting eyes upon them;
   without acting, he accomplishes great things.

A Chinese commentator says:

"Such is the essence of our nature, that it embraces and traverses the whole
universe; it knows neither distance nor nearness of time or space. The saint knows
everything without passing through his door or opening his window, because his
nature is absolutely perfect; but men of the world are blinded by material things,
their nature is limited by the limits of the senses; they are perturbed by their bodies
and their emotions. Outwardly they are stopped by mountains and rivers, they see
not beyond the scope of their eyes, they hear not beyond the reach of their ears.
The slightest obstacle may paralyse either of these faculties."

Lao Tzu's thought appears to be exactly that of the sentences in *Isha Upanishad:*

"Without moving, that One is swifter than mind. Nor did the bright Powers
overtake It; It went swiftly before them. That outstrips the others, though they
run, while It stands still."[57]

48

He who gives himself to studies, each day increases (his information).
He who gives himself to the Way, each day diminishes (his desires).
He diminishes them continually until he attains non-action.
When he has attained non-action all things are possible for him.
Through non-action he becomes master of the kingdom.
He who follows action cannot become master of the kingdom.

The Chinese phrase *wu-wei* is here translated non-action; its meaning is: abstinence
from action inspired by selfishness; just as it has been said that we should do nothing
which is desired by the lower self for that reason alone.

The whole matter is set forth at length in the *Bhagavad Gita*, and is, indeed, the most
distinctive teaching of that Scripture of detachment and disinterested toil.

The Sanskrit word involved is *karma*. It may be interesting to try the experiment of
re-writing Lao Tzu's phrases, using this word:

"He who gives himself to the Way, each day diminishes his evil desires. He diminishes
them continually until he attains freedom from karma. When he has attained to freedom
from karma all things become possible for him. Through liberation from karma he
becomes master of the kingdom of heaven. He who is bound by karma cannot become
master of the kingdom of heaven."

This is exactly the teaching of the closing passage of *Light on the Path:*

"The operations of the actual laws of karma are not to be studied until the disciple has reached the point at which they no longer affect himself. . . . Therefore you who desire to understand the laws of karma, attempt first to free yourself from these laws; and this can only be done by fixing your attention on that which is unaffected by them."[58]

49

The sage has no set mental forms. He adapts himself to the minds of the people.
With the good, he is good; with the evil, he is also good.
This is the perfection of goodness.
With the sincere, he is sincere; with the insincere, he is also sincere. This is the perfection of sincerity.
The holy sage, living in the world, dwells serene and unperturbed, keeping the same feeling for all.
The hundred families follow him with their ears and eyes.
The sage regards them as his children.

The best comment seems to be the following passage, quoted from the Revised Version:

"Ye have heard that it was said, Thou shalt love thy neighbour, and hate thine enemy: but I say unto you, Love your enemies, and pray for them that persecute you; that ye may be sons of your Father which is in heaven: for he maketh his sun to rise on the evil and the good, and sendeth rain on the just and the unjust. . . . Ye therefore shall be perfect, as your heavenly Father is perfect."[59]

Here is another memorable phrase: "The men of old said: All men seek to conquer death; they do not know how to conquer life."

50

Man departs from life to enter into death.
There are thirteen causes of life and thirteen causes of death.
No sooner is the man born, than these thirteen causes of death drag him swiftly toward his end.
What is the reason? It is because he desires to live too impetuously.
But I have learnt that he who rightly rules his life fears neither rhinoceros nor tiger in his path.
He enters the host and needs neither breastplate nor sword.
The rhinoceros finds no unguarded place to pierce with his horn, nor the tiger to tear him with its claws,
    nor the soldier to pierce him with his sword.
What is the cause? There is no place of death in him.

Commenting on the second line, one of the Chinese commentators says:

"There are thirteen causes of life, that is, thirteen means for reaching spiritual life, namely: Emptiness of self, attachment to non-action, purity, quietude, humility, poverty, gentleness, tenderness, lowliness, simplicity, modesty, docility, economy. There are thirteen causes of death, which are the opposites of these, namely: Being filled with self, attachment to creatures, impurity, agitation, vanity, wealth, hardness, violence, pride, lavishness, haughtiness, rigidity, prodigality."

Of the next sentences, a commentator says:

"Lao Tzu is speaking here of worldly men, who are passionately attached to worldly life and who know not the Way. How comes it that, thirstily seeking happiness, they find misery? It is because they work only to satisfy their passions and their personal interests; they do not know that, the more ardently they pursue the things of this life, the closer they come to death."

Another commentator adds:

"One of the men of old said: He who loves his life may be killed; he who is self-righteous may be soiled; he who thirsts for fame may be covered with shame; he who seeks perfection for himself may lose it. But if he stand apart from bodily life, who can kill him? If he stand apart from self-righteousness, who can soil him? If he stand apart from fame, who can put him to shame? If he seek not perfection for himself, who can make him lose it? He who understands this, has risen above life and death."

51

The Way produces beings; righteousness nourishes them. These two give them a
  body and perfect them through a secret impulsion.
This is why all beings revere the Way and honour righteousness.
None conferred on the Way its dignity, nor on righteousness its nobility: they
  possess them eternally in themselves.
This is why the Way produces beings, nourishes them, increases them, perfects
  them, ripens them, feeds them, protects them.
It produces them, but does not appropriate them;
  It makes them what they are, but does not therefore exalt itself;
  It reigns over them and leaves them free.
This is what is called perfect righteousness.

The righteousness of which Lao Tzu speaks here, says a Chinese commentator, is the manifestation of the Way in creatures. The Way expands like a river; it manifests itself outwardly, and becomes righteousness. When unmanifested, immaterial, void, it is called the Way; when it transforms and nourishes creatures, it is called righteousness.

Another commentator finds a striking parallel for the secret impulsion of the Way and of righteousness: By the force of impulsion, they perfect beings and lead them to their complete development. In the same way, if the force of Spring impels plants, they cannot resist coming to birth; if the force of Autumn impels them, they cannot resist coming to maturity. There is no being, says the same commentator, which from its birth to its complete development does not need the Way and righteousness. This is why all beings honour and revere them. There is no being that brings its nobility with it at birth. In order that the Emperor may be revered and surrounded with honours, he must have been consecrated by Heaven; that his vassals may be revered and surrounded with honours, they must have been appointed by the Emperor. But the Way and righteousness have no need that any should confer on them their dignity and their nobility; they are honourable of themselves.

The ruler of the kingdom, says a third commentator, must find all his glory in adhering closely to the Way and in emptying his heart, in order to attain to the perfection of righteousness.

52

The Principle of the world became the Mother of the world.

Gaining the Mother, one knows her children.

He who knows the children and retains their Mother, to the end of his days is exposed to no danger.

If he close his mouth, if he shut his ears and eyes, to the end of his days he shall feel no weariness.

But if he open his mouth and increase his desires, to the end of his life he cannot be saved.

He who sees the most subtle things is called enlightened;
  he who preserves his weakness is called strong.

He who uses the brightness of the Way and returns to its light, need fear no bodily calamity.

He is said to be doubly enlightened.

"Before the Way had a name," says the commentator, "beings received their principle from It; when It had a name, they received their life from It. This is why the Way is first called Principle, and afterwards Mother. The words, 'her children,' designate all beings. The Saint knows all beings, because he identifies himself with the Way, just as through the mother one knows the children. But, though his rare insight allows him to penetrate all beings, beings must never make him forget the Way. This is why to the end of his life he retains the Mother. The misfortune of the worldly is to forget the Way, through ardently seeking those things which flatter their senses."

Concerning the shutting of the ears and eyes, a commentator says:

"If a man allow himself to be drawn away by the enjoyment of music or the love of beauty, and forget to retrace his steps, he pursues beings and revolts against his nature. Therefore he should inwardly concentrate his hearing and his sight. Therefore Lao Tzu advises him to dose his ears and eyes, in order that outward things may not enter into his soul. If he act thus, through his whole life he may use the Way, never suffering weariness. But if he gave himself up to the desires which flatter the ears and the eyes, if he let himself be drawn away by the impetuousness of the senses without returning to the good way, he would lose his heart under the influence of beings and, to the end of his life, he could not be saved."

With this we may compare the sentences of *Light on the Path:*

"Before the eyes can see they must be incapable of tears. Before the ear can hear it must have lost its sensitiveness."[60]

Concerning enlightenment by the light of the Way, a commentator says:

"The Way may be considered as a tree of which its light is the root, and the emanation of its light, the branches. These branches spread themselves forth and produce in man the faculty of seeing, hearing, feeling, perceiving. The Way flows from the root to the branches. Enlightenment sets forth from the branches to seek the root. This is why Lao Tzu says: 'He who uses the brightness of the Way to return to its light, is called doubly enlightened.'"

53

If I were endowed with perception, I would walk in the great Way.
The one thing that I fear is to be involved in action.
The great Way is one, but the people love by-ways.
If the palaces are splendid, the fields are untilled, the granaries are empty.
The princes are adorned with magnificent fabrics;
    they carry a sharp sword;
    they fill themselves with exquisite banquets;
    they are puffed up with riches.
This is what is called glorifying themselves through theft;
    it is not to follow the Way.

In the second sentence of the text, "to be involved in action" means, to be bound by the bonds of Karma. The cure is detachment: to do the right because it is the right, without thought of personal gain or loss.

For the fourth and following sentences, the best commentary is the saying, "All that ever came before me are thieves and robbers."[61] This is said to be the echo of a sentence in a ritual of Initiation. The spiritual Self, awakened and coming into his kingdom, sees that the personal selves that went before, the selves of egotism and sensual desire, were thieves and robbers, plundering and impoverishing the spiritual nature; prostituting divine powers and gifts for self-indulgence. In Lao Tzu's words, "This is what is called glorifying themselves through theft."

54

He who knows how to establish, fears not destruction;
    he who knows how to preserve, fears not to lose.
His sons and grandsons will offer sacrifices to him in unbroken succession.
If he follow the Way within himself, his righteousness will become pure.
If he cultivate it in his family, his righteousness will become abounding.
If he cultivate it in the village, his righteousness will become extended.

If he cultivate it in the province, his righteousness will become flourishing.
If he cultivate it in the kingdom, his righteousness will become universal.
This is why I judge other men after myself;
   I judge other families after one family;
   I judge other villages after one village;
   I judge other provinces after one province;
   I judge the kingdom after the kingdom.
How do I know that it is thus with the kingdom?
   I know it solely by that (Way).

The Chinese commentator says that, if one plant a tree on a plain, a time will surely come when it will be torn up and thrown down. But that which is rightly established is never torn up. If one hold an object between his hands, a moment will surely come when he will let it go. But that which we rightly preserve will never escape us. This double comparison refers to him who is established in righteousness and firmly keeps the Way.

We may cite in comparison:

"Whosoever heareth these sayings of mine, and doeth them, I will liken him unto a wise man, which built his house upon a rock."[62]

It would seem that the "sons and grandsons" are spiritual descendants, disciples of a Master of Wisdom, and that the sentences that follow may be taken to indicate the widening outlook of the disciple as he ascends from the branches toward the root of that tree of light, rooted in Heaven, which is the Way. Beginning by seeking the Way within himself, and looking within his own heart for the light, he is presently able to recognize that light in the hearts of others, a group of co-disciples, his own spiritual family. And so onward, until he becomes a Master of the kingdom.

55

He who possesses firmly established righteousness is like a child new born, who
   fears neither the stings of poisonous creatures, nor the claws of wild beasts,
   nor the talons of birds of prey.
His bones are weak, his muscles are soft, and yet he seizes objects firmly.
He is without the passions of sex, yet there is creative power within him. This
   comes from the perfection of the life-force.
The new-born will cry all day without losing his voice; this comes from the
   perfection of harmony in his powers.
To know harmony is to be firmly established.
To be firmly established is to be enlightened.
To extend his life outward is calamity.
When the impulse of vital energy springs from the heart, this is called strength.
When beings have thus reached their full growth, they begin to grow old.
This is what is called failure to follow the Way.
He who follows not the Way, soon perishes.

Lao Tzu is here speaking of the birth of the spiritual man, of whom it is said:

"Except a man be born again, he cannot see the kingdom of God; except a man be born of water and the Spirit, he cannot enter into the kingdom of God."[63]

The stinging, poisonous creature from whom the spiritual man is set free, is the snake of the lower self; the wild beasts are the passions; the birds of prey are the harpies of evil desires.

It is a quaint simile, the new-born child crying all day with unwearied voice; the thought appears to be the power of the spiritual man to "toil terribly," with spiritual second wind.

To be firmly established is to be enlightened: "He who is perfected in devotion finds wisdom springing up within him."[64] Then comes the contrast, where all the vital impulses go outward after sensual aims, and the heart is filled with impetuous desires. On the heels of that strength come decay and death.

56

The man who knows the Way speaks not; he who speaks knows it not.

He closes his lips, he shuts his ears and eyes, he controls his activity, he frees himself from all bonds, he tempers his light, he seems as one of the multitude.

He may be said to be like the Way.

He is untouched by favour as by disgrace, by loss as by gain, by honour as by dishonour.

This is why he is the most honourable man under heaven.

The commentator says that the Saint keeps himself in calm and silence. He restrains the intemperance of the tongue. He pays no heed to the things which may flatter the ears and eyes. He concentrates inwardly his power of seeing and hearing.

He tempers his light; he brings light, but without dazzling anyone, giving to each the light he can receive. As he has few desires, the commentator adds, and few private interests, he cannot be rewarded; as he possesses the fullness of righteousness, he cannot be harmed; as he desires neither the favour of princes nor glory, he cannot be honoured; as he shrinks not from lowliness and abjection, he cannot be abased. This is the character of perfect righteousness; therefore he is the most honourable man under heaven.

Or, as an English poet has said of one who was thus perfected in righteousness, he was "the first true gentleman that ever breathed."[65]

57

With rectitude he governs the realm; with strategy he makes war; with detachment in action he becomes master of the kingdom.

How do I know that it is thus with the kingdom? By this:

The more the ruler multiplies interdictions and restrictions,
    the poorer become the people;

The more the people seek means of wealth,
    the more the realm is disturbed;

The more the people gain of craft and subtlety,
    the more fantastic possessions are multiplied;

The more the laws are complicated, the more robbers increase.

Therefore the Saint says: I practise detachment in action, and the people are
  converted spontaneously.
I love quietude, and the people become righteous of their own accord.
I do not busy myself, and the people spontaneously grow rich.
I free myself from desires, and the people of themselves return to simplicity.

The present commentator is inclined to think that Lao Tzu has in mind a contrast
between two methods of religious training: on the one hand, such a system of multiplied
commands and restrictions as that of the Pharisees; on the other, such an Order as that
instituted by the Buddha, with renunciation of all possessions and all worldly activities, in
order to secure inwardness and quietude of heart. There may be a reconciliation of the two
which, with complete detachment and devotion, combines an ordered discipline of all the
powers, and it would seem certain that, on the inner side of his Order, the Buddha
perfected such a discipline.

58

When the government does not scrutinize too closely, the people become rich.
When the government is inquisitorial, the people lack all things.
Happiness is born from misfortune; misfortune is hidden in the heart of
  happiness. Who can foresee the outcome?
If the prince be not upright, upright men become deceitful, and righteous men
  perverse.
Men are plunged in errors, and this has already lasted long.
This is why the Saint is just, and injures not.
He is disinterested and harms not.
He is upright and does not chastise.
He is enlightened and does not dazzle.

The Chinese commentators are inclined to take this and the preceding, as well as the
two following sections as aphorisms of practical politics, in the general sense of "less
government in business," and modern students of excessive government intervention may
find much to agree with in this view.

But it seems to the present commentator that Lao Tzu, while he may have been
considering and criticizing the interfering and meticulous princes of his time, had also in
mind something deeper; some such contrast as that between the legalistic Brahmans and
the simplicity of the Buddha, or what Paul had in mind when he set faith against the
works of the law.

The Chinese commentators go deeper when they take up the sentence: Happiness is
born of misfortune. One of them declares that, when a man has fallen into some
calamity, if he be able to repent of his faults, diligently to examine himself, and to be
ceaselessly vigilant, he changes his misfortune into happiness. But when, on the contrary,
a man sees all his desires fulfilled, if he grow haughty, abandoning himself to his passions
without thinking of returning to righteousness, a host of misfortunes will descend upon
him.

The same commentator, considering later sentences in this section, says that it is not only since yesterday that men are blind, abandoning rectitude. This blindness comes on insensibly; their misfortune is, that they are unconscious of it. This is why the Saint is careful of even the least things; he is always fearful that the people may come to destruction. Unjust and greedy men become just and disinterested under the influence of the Saint's example, so that he has no need to punish them.

There is much in this part of Lao Tzu's work that suggests the sentences:

"He shall not strive, nor cry; neither shall any man hear his voice in the streets. A bruised reed shall he not break, and smoking flax shall he not quench, till he send forth judgement unto victory."[66]

59

To govern men and serve Heaven, nothing can be compared to moderation.
Moderation should be the first care of man.
When it has become his first care, it may be said that
    he is storing up righteousness abundantly.
When he stores up righteousness abundantly,
    there is nothing that he does not overcome.
When there is nothing that he does not overcome,
    no one knows his limits.
When no one knows his limits, he is able to possess the kingdom.
He who possesses the Mother of the kingdom maintains himself long.
This is to be deeply rooted, and to have a well set stem.
This is the way of long life and an existence that endures.

The Chinese commentators suppose that by moderation Lao Tzu here means a wise governance both of outward possessions and of the inner powers of one's nature. One of them holds that the sovereign virtue, which is the Mother of the kingdom, is indeed the spirit and method of the Way. He who conforms himself to the spirit of the Way, the divine light that shines from above, both governs men and serves heaven.

Beginning to follow the Way, making the profound obeisance of the soul to the dim star that burns within, in the fullness of time he is able to possess the kingdom; rooted in the Eternal, he is conformed to the life of the Eternal and inherits eternal life.

60

To govern a great kingdom, one should imitate him who cooks a little fish.
When the ruler governs the kingdom according to the Way, the spirits do not
    show their power.
It is not that the demons lack power, but that the demons do not injure men.
It is not that the spirits cannot injure men, but that the Saint himself does not
    injure men.
Neither the Saint nor the spirits injure them; this is why their power is blended.

The simile in the first sentence, concerning the great kingdom and the little fish, has the same rather startling quaintness as a former simile for the impartiality of Heaven and Earth, which "regard all creatures as men regard the straw dogs"[67] used in sacrifice. If we accept the text as being what Lao Tzu actually wrote, we may imagine him watching some peasant woman cooking little fish, handling them somewhat daintily, careful that they shall be cooked enough, but not too much; and saying to himself, or perhaps even to her: "That is exactly how a kingdom should be governed, with tact and discretion!"

There may be much more than our skeptical day and generation would willingly believe, in Lao Tzu's thought that spirits are subject to the Saint; natural forces which we think of as merely mechanical, may have something of consciousness, and a consciousness responsive to the divine powers in man, so that "even the winds and the sea obey him."[68]

61

The great kingdom shall be as the rivers and the seas, in which all the waters
    under heaven are united.
In the world, this is the part of the feminine:
    through quietude it constantly triumphs over the masculine. This quietude is
    a kind of abasement.
This is why, if the great kingdom abase itself before the little kingdoms, it will
    win the little kingdoms.
If the little kingdoms abase themselves before the great kingdom, they will win
    the great kingdom.
This is why some abase themselves in order to receive, while others abase
    themselves in order to be received.
The great kingdom desires only to unite and guide mankind.
The little kingdom desires only to be permitted to serve mankind.
Therefore both obtain what they desire.
But the great must abase themselves.

If the teaching of Lao Tzu in many ways approaches the spirit of Christianity, this is, perhaps, the most distinctively Christian section in the whole work. We have not only the often repeated saying of the Master Christ, "He that shall humble himself shall be exalted,"[69] but the example of the Master, "who, being in the form of God, counted it not a thing to be grasped to be on an equality with God, but emptied himself, taking the form of a bond-servant, being made in the likeness of men; and being found in fashion as a man, he humbled himself, becoming obedient even unto death, yea, the death of the Cross. Wherefore also God highly exalted him."[70]

We may believe that the Master Christ made himself pitiful, because pity is the final appeal to hard and self-centred human hearts, and that self-abasement in order to make this appeal is of the essence of his sacrifice. And we may also believe that what the Master Christ did visibly, all Masters do in the invisible world, making themselves bond-servants of mankind.

We have often found reason to believe that, when Lao Tzu speaks of "the great kingdom," he means the spiritual kingdom, the Lodge of Masters. And it would seem that "the little kingdom" here means mankind, and also the individual disciple. We can thus see a very real meaning in the saying that, "if the great kingdom abase itself before the little kingdom, it will win the little kingdom"; and, if "the little kingdom" means the disciple, then it is profoundly true that "the little kingdom desires only to be permitted to serve."

62

The Way is the refuge of all beings; it is the treasure of the righteous man and
   the support of the wicked.
Excellent words can bring us riches, honourable acts can lift us above others.
If a man be not righteous, should he be driven away with contempt?
For his sake the Emperor was established and the three ministers were appointed.
It is good to hold up a tablet of jade, or to mount a chariot with four horses; but
   it is better to remain still, in order to advance in the Way.
Why did the ancients esteem the Way?
Is it not because the Way is found daily without seeking?
Is it not because the guilty gain through It liberty and life?
This is why the Way is the noblest thing in the world.

Here again we have ideas in entire harmony with the teaching of Christ:

"But go ye and learn what this meaneth, I desire mercy, and not sacrifice: for I came not to call the righteous, but sinners."[71]

That this is the meaning attributed to the words of Lao Tzu by his followers is shown by the commentary:

"If a man has faults, it is enough for him to amend in order to become righteous. This is why he should not be driven away because of his faults. If, in antiquity, the Emperor and three ministers were established, it was precisely in order to instruct and reform the vicious."

The tradition is, that the minister held a tablet of jade before his face when he entered the Emperor's presence; to hold up a tablet of jade thus means to enter the presence of the Emperor.

Regarding the closing sentences, the commentators say:

"The wise men of old did not make long journeys in search of the Way; they returned to their pristine purity and found It within themselves."

63

The wise man works without working,
   he is employed without being employed,
   he savours that which is without savour.
Great things or small things, many or few, are equal in his eyes.
He repays injuries with kindness.
He begins with easy things when considering hard things;
   with little things when planning great things.

The hardest things in the world began of necessity by being easy.
The greatest things in the world began of necessity by being small.
Therefore the Saint seeks not at all to do great things; this is why he can
    accomplish great things.
He who promises lightly, rarely keeps his word.
He who finds many things easy, of necessity meets many difficulties.
Therefore the Saint finds all things difficult; this is why, to his life's end, he
    meets with no difficulties.

The principle of detachment has already been considered. Of the later sentences, a
commentator says:

"Among the men of the world, there is not one who does not fear great things
and disdain little things. It is only when things have become difficult that he plans
them, and when they have become great that he undertakes them, and he
continually fails. The Saint puts on the same level things great and small, many
and few; he fears all equally; he finds them all equally difficult. How could he fail
to succeed?"

Another commentator says:

"A difficult thing did not become difficult all at once; it is born of easy things,
and, through the insensible accumulation of these, it becomes difficult. This is why
he who plans difficult things, must begin with what is easy in them. Great things
did not become great all at once. They began by being little, and, by gradual
progression and growth, they became great. This is why he who desires to
accomplish a great thing, must begin with what is little in it. The Saint never seeks
to accomplish great things all at once; he is content to accumulate little things;
this is why he comes to accomplish great things."

64

What is at rest is easy to maintain;
    what has not yet appeared is easy to guard against;
    what is weak is easy to break; what is small is easy to scatter.
Stop the evil before it exists; quiet the disorder before it arises.
A tree of mighty trunk springs from a root as thin as a hair;
    a tower nine stories high began in a handful of clay;
    a journey of a thousand miles began with one step.
He who is absorbed in action fails;
    he who attaches himself to anything loses it.
Therefore the Saint is not absorbed in action, and does not fail.
He attaches himself to nothing, and loses nothing.
When the men of the world undertake anything, it always fails at the moment
    of success.
Pay heed to the end as well as to the beginning, and you will never fail.
Therefore the Saint makes his desire consist in the absence of all desire. He does

not long for possessions that are difficult to gain.

He is zealous to be free from zeal, and escapes the faults of other men.

He guards himself against becoming absorbed in work, in order that he may help all beings to follow out their law.

The words "what is at rest," says a commentator, indicate the time when no thought has yet been born in the heart, when joy or wrath have not yet shown themselves on the countenance, when the soul is perfectly serene and free from all emotion.

Regarding the simile of the tree, a commentator says:

"This comparison shows that little things are the origin of great. If you wish to remove a tree, you must begin by tearing up the roots, otherwise it will grow again. If you wish to stop the flow of water, you must control the spring, otherwise it will flow anew. If you wish to end an evil, you must stop its source, otherwise it will burst forth once more."

Regarding a later sentence a commentator says:

"When common men see that an undertaking is on the point of succeeding, they yield to negligence and levity; then the undertaking changes its face, and they fail completely. Be on the watch, therefore, at the end of your undertakings, as men are at the beginning; then you will be able to bring them to perfect accomplishment and will never fail."

Of the last sentence of the text a commentator says:

"All beings have their proper nature. The men of the multitude do not follow the purity of their nature; they change themselves by giving themselves up to a disordered activity. They abandon candour and simplicity, to follow after cunning and astuteness; they give up what is easy and simple, to run after things arduous and complicated. In this they sin. The Saint sets himself to do the opposite."

65

In antiquity, those who excelled in following the Way did not use it to enlighten the people; they used it to keep the people simple and ignorant.

The people is hard to govern because it has too much astuteness.

He who makes use of astuteness to govern the kingdom,
    is the scourge of the kingdom.

He who does not use astuteness to govern the kingdom,
    brings happiness to the kingdom.

When a man knows these two things, he is the model.

To know how to be the model, is to be endowed with heavenly virtue.

This heavenly virtue is deep, measureless, opposed to creatures.

By it he succeeds in gaining wide-extended peace.

"When the people," says a commentator, "has not lost its simple and candid nature, it is easy to instruct and convert it; when the sincerity of its feelings has not been changed, it is easy to make it obey the laws. But as soon as it has gained much astuteness, its purity and simplicity vanish, while craft and hypocrisy grow in it from day to day. If one should wish to teach the people the Way, and to make it adopt upright and orderly conduct, he will meet with immense difficulties. This is the reason why the wise men of antiquity sought to keep the people simple and ignorant, instead of enlightening it."

To put the matter in another way, the men of old thought that moral training should come before mental instruction.

66

Why are the rivers and the seas able to be the lords of all waters?
Because they know how to put themselves below them.
Because of this, they are able to become the lords of all waters.
So when the Saint wishes to rule the people, he must, by his words,
　　put himself below the people.
When he desires to be placed in front of the people, he must
　　put himself after the people.
So it comes that the Saint is set above the people,
　　yet does not become a burden to the people;
　　he is placed before all and the people suffers no hurt.
Thus all under heaven loves to serve him and does not weary of him.
As he does not claim precedence, there is none under heaven who can go
　　before him.

"All the streams of the world," says the commentator, "enter the rivers and the seas, giving themselves up to them; this is why the rivers and the seas are the lords of all streams. How do they bring the streams to them? Only because they are below them."

One wonders whether, in those distant days, the people did in any general sense honour and obey the lowly and meek. It would seem to be the supreme sacrifice of the Masters, that, to help mankind, they must put themselves at the mercy of mankind; and mankind has as yet so little mercy.

67

All the world says my path is lofty, yet I am as one of low degree.
It is only because my path is mighty that I am as one of low degree.
As for the intelligent, their littleness has long been recognised.
I am the possessor of three precious things: I hold them and guard them as a
　　treasure.
The first is called love; the second is called economy; the third is called humility,
　　which forbids me to wish to be first under heaven.
I have love, and therefore I can be courageous.
I have economy, and therefore I can spend largely.
I dare not wish to be the first under heaven, therefore I can become the leader of

all men.
But to-day they neglect love, to follow rashness;
 they neglect economy and spend largely;
 they neglect the lower place, to seek the higher place.
This path leads to death.
He who engages in warfare with a heart full of love gains the victory;
 if the city be guarded, it cannot be taken.
Whom Heaven would save, to him It gives love as a protection.

Perhaps the essence of this section may be summed up in the words: "He that hateth his life in this world shall keep it unto life eternal."[72] The Greek word means the psychical life.[73] He who hates the psychical, self-assertive principle in himself, guards his true life in the Eternal. This is a lofty path, yet he must be lowly who would tread it.

The three treasures are the reward of treading this path. Love is the life-breath of the Eternal, which breathes through the spiritual man, inspiring him with supreme courage to work for the purposes of the Eternal, and therefore to work courageously against the forces of self-assertion and self-seeking which seek to rob the Eternal. Economy is the wise use of all powers and resources, including the powers of the spiritual man; the right use of small efforts and small spaces of time. He who uses the moments for the Eternal, has time for much. He can spend and be spent for the purposes of the Eternal. Humility is to see oneself as being a part of the Eternal, having life only through the Eternal, seeking no purposes but the purposes of the Eternal. It is to burn up once for all the poisonous desire "to be the first under heaven," which is, whether avowed or not, the impulse of the lower self in every one; to surrender the heart utterly to the Eternal, in the spirit of reverent worship; and, in every thought and effort, to seek not self but the Eternal.

68

The excellent leader of armies is free from the spirit of contention.
The excellent warrior does not yield to wrath.
The excellent conqueror strives not.
The excellent leader of men puts himself below them.
This is called the possession of righteousness without contention.
This is called the wisdom to guide the powers of men.
This is called union with Heaven.
Such was the sublime wisdom of the ancients.

It is once more a question of the spiritual man inspired by the life-breath of the Eternal. He works valiantly and unweariedly for the purposes of the Eternal, yet he is free from the spirit of contention and wrath. He neither strives nor cries.

But, since the powers of the Eternal which inspire him dwell also in the hearts of other men, giving them all the life that they possess, he who understands and serves these forces can guide others into the way of righteousness.

69

A warrior of the ancients has said:
I dare not give the signal, as does the host; I had rather receive it, as does the guest.
I dare not advance an inch, I had rather withdraw a foot.
This is to have no rank to follow, no arm to stretch out, no enemy to pursue, no
    weapon to seize.
There is no greater error than to make light of the enemy.
To make light of the enemy is almost to lose our treasure.
Therefore, when two equally equipped armies meet, he who has the most love
    wins the victory.

According to one of the Chinese commentaries, this section is to be understood figuratively. It is intended to describe the humility and reserve of those who follow the Way.

Perhaps we shall be right, if we think of it as covering the same ground as certain sentences in *Light on the Path*: "Stand aside in the coming battle, and though thou fightest be not thou the warrior";[74] "seek the way by retreating within."[75] The disciple is bidden to fasten the energies of the soul upon the task, the attitude opposite to making light of the determined and pitiless enemy. Carrying on the same thought, we may say that, in the conflict between the higher and lower nature, which is really a fight to the death, the higher nature wins because it has the greater love, love of the Eternal, as against self-love.

70

My words are easy to understand, easy to carry out.
In the world, none can understand them, none can carry them out.
My words have a source, my acts have a rule.
Men understand them not, and therefore know me not.
Those who understand me are few, yet am I the more honoured.
Therefore the Saint is plainly clad, and carries his jewels in his bosom.

The commentator says that the source of the Sage's words is the Way, that the rule of his acts is Righteousness, the practical following of the Way. Through the Way and Righteousness the Saint directs all the business of the kingdom, through them he clearly discerns success and failure, what is worthy of praise and what is worthy of blame; through them he distinguishes the portents of ill fortune and good fortune, of victory and defeat. Thus the Way is the source of his words, and Righteousness is the rule of his acts.

The last phrase in the text seems fairly paraphrased by the words:

"That power which the disciple shall covet is that which shall make him appear as nothing in the eyes of men."[76]

One of the Chinese commentators has this to say of it:

"Inwardly, the Saint possesses sublime beauty; but, in his outward mien, he seems common and dull. He is like the oyster that hides a pearl under its rough shell; like the rude matrix that conceals a precious diamond. Therefore the herd cannot perceive his inner beauty or his hidden virtues."

71

To know, and to think that we know not, is the crown.
Not to know, and to think we know, is the affliction.
If you are afflicted by this affliction, then you will not experience it.
The Saint does not experience this affliction, because he is afflicted by it.
This is why he does not experience it.

The Chinese commentators thus explain this paradox: To know the Way, and to say we know It not, is the crown of righteousness. To be dazzled by the knowledge which is born of contact with things sensible, and not to possess the non-knowledge which constitutes true knowledge, is the general defect of the men of this world. He who knows not the Way is attached to false knowledge, which he mistakes for real knowledge. When false knowledge occupies his soul, it becomes an afflicting sickness. False knowledge is the afflicting sickness of our nature. When a man knows that false knowledge is an afflicting sickness, and is afflicted by this, then he no longer experiences the afflicting sickness of false knowledge. To know the Way, and to know that he knows It not, is the condition of the Saint. The Saint is free from the afflicting sickness of false knowledge. This is why the afflicting sickness of false knowledge departs from him.

Perhaps we might put the same thought in another way: Real wisdom must always include a recognition of the great Mystery, the Unknowable. The Saint may know God; he cannot know why God is, or why He is Love. But he who is subject to the world-glamour of Maya,[77] and is, therefore, continuously deceived, believes that he is facing realities. That very belief is the root of his delusion. But to recognize glamour, and to resent the tyranny of glamour, is to begin to free oneself from glamour. The Saint fights against the tyranny of glamour; therefore he is not the thrall of glamour.

72

When the people fear not what should be feared, then what is most to be feared
    descends upon them.
Beware of thinking your dwelling too narrow;
    beware of resentment over your lot.
I resent not my lot, therefore I find no cause for resentment in it.
Hence the Saint knows himself and does not make himself conspicuous;
    he exercises restraint and does not glorify himself.
This is why he shuns the one and follows the other.

In the course of life, say the commentators, the people have not the sense to fear what should be feared; they yield to their inclinations and indulge their passions, thinking there is no harm in this. Soon vices grow until they cannot be hidden, and crimes increase so that they cannot free themselves from them; then comes death, the thing most to be feared.

Your house may be low, or it may be lofty; in either, you can find content. Beware of thinking your house too small and narrow, as though it could not contain you. Your means may be abundant or restricted. In either case they will meet your needs. Beware of thinking them less than your deserts. Common people do not understand their destiny, and therefore they resent their lot. The Saint alone knows himself and his state, and gladly accepts the lot which Heaven sends him; he boasts not nor seeks outward things, and therefore he has enough. Common people are dissatisfied with their dwellings and think them narrow. But the Saint loves his home, and is everywhere content. He is not great in his own eyes, and seeks not to shine in the eyes of others.

Here again we may suggest a deeper meaning: Maya, glamour, personal delusion, is the root evil; he who is led by glamour is subject to death. The Saint, who has found his home in spiritual reality, understands and accepts his life as a part of spiritual reality. He resents nothing and is full of humility, knowing that he exists only through the grace of Divine Law.

73

He who dares to disobey, finds death.
He who dares to obey, finds life.
Of these two, one is helpful, one is hurtful.
When Heaven is offended, who can know the cause?
Therefore the Saint acts circumspectly.
This is the Way of Heaven:
It strives not, yet wins the victory.
It speaks not, yet wins obedience.
It calls not, yet men hasten thither.
It seems to delay, yet Its plans are wise.
The net of Heaven is spread out, its meshes are wide, yet none escapes it.

He who follows the headstrong lower self rashly disobeys the divine law, and takes the path of death. He who dares to control the lower self, thereby obeys divine law, and takes the path of life. He who follows the headstrong leading of the lower self, and thereby violates divine law, feels the penalty but does not recognize the reason why he is punished. But the Saint diligently seeks to understand divine law, and to obey it.

The Way, the Logos, works silently, guiding all life, and winning always; divine law is always triumphant. The powers of the Logos work slowly through immense periods of time, yet always toward the defined goal, the redemption of mankind and all life. None evades the meshes of divine law.

74

If the people fear not death, they will not be frightened by the threat of death.
If the people constantly fear death, and one of them does evil, then I can seize
    him and put him to death, so that none will dare to imitate him.
There is always a supreme authority to inflict death.
If anyone wish to usurp the place of this supreme authority, and himself inflict
    death, he is like one who wishes to cut wood in the place of the carpenter.
When one wishes to cut wood in the place of the carpenter, it is rarely that he
    wounds not his own hands.

The Chinese commentators take this literally, as a criticism of their criminal law: when death is the punishment for every fault, people no longer fear death. But we may find a deeper meaning, by following out the thought of the preceding section: the Logos in action, as the law of Karma, rules all life and adjusts all violation of law by what appears as punishment, but is really spiritual education. Those who do not realize the action of Karma, because they are blinded by the lower self, do not abstain from evil. They are not restrained by the fear of violating the law, because they do not realize the existence of the law. But those who realize the law are deterred from evil through fear of violating that law. On the other hand, those who try to "take the law into their own hands" and to influence others while ignorant of their Karma, which means their real needs, are certain to "cut their own fingers."

75

The people hunger because the prince consumes the produce of the land.
This is why the people hunger.
The people are hard to govern because the prince is too active.
This is why they are hard to govern.
The people despise death, because they seek the means of life too eagerly.
This is why they despise death.
But he who is not over busy with life is wiser than he who esteems life.

Once again the commentators take Lao Tzu's meaning to be a criticism of political conditions. But it seems equally possible that his meaning is symbolical: the powers of the whole nature starve because the lower self usurps the field and appropriates the life forces. The powers are hard to control because the lower self is too active. The powers despise death and rush headlong into danger, because of the lower self's thirst for sensations and emotions. But he who is detached from life and does not seek sensations or emotions, is wiser than he who is immersed in life.

76

When a man is born, he is supple and weak;
   when he dies, he is strong and rigid.
When trees and plants first spring up, they are pliable and tender;
   when they die, they are dry and hard.
Hardness and force are the attendants of death;
   suppleness and weakness are the attendants of life.
This is why, when the army is strong, it does not win the victory.
When a tree has grown strong, it is cut down.
He who is strong and great occupies the lower rank;
   he who is pliable and weak occupies the higher rank.

A wise Chinese commentator says that this whole section has a symbolical meaning. Lao Tzu wishes to say that he who draws near to the Way through yielding and obedience, is assured of life, and he who departs from the Way, seeking force and power, and striving against obstacles instead of yielding to them, will perish without fail.

This seems to be another version of the saying that he who will save his life shall lose it, but he who will lose his life shall save it, keeping it unto life eternal.[78]

77

The Way of Heaven is like the maker of a bow, who lowers what is high and raises what is low; who removes excess and supplies what is lacking.

Heaven takes the excess of those who have it, in order to help those who are lacking.

It is not so with men, who take from those who lack, to give to those who have in excess.

Who can give from his abundance to all who are under Heaven? He alone, who possesses the Way.

Therefore the Saint does good without glorying in it.

He accomplishes great things, but is detached from them.

He does not wish his wisdom to be seen.

Heaven, says a commentator, seeks to bring about a balance in all things, taking the excess of some, and supplying the lack of others. Man is in opposition to Heaven, and does not follow the law of balance. He alone who possesses the Way understands the way of Heaven. The wise men of old who surpassed others, used their powers for the good of others.

Again, we may perhaps find a deeper meaning: the lower self, which is in excess, is to be diminished; the better self, which at present is deprived of its part in life, is to be made strong. This victory will mean humility, detachment, and a blessing to others.

78

Nothing under Heaven is softer and weaker than water, yet nothing can better break what is hard and strong.

In this, nothing can take the place of water.

The weak triumphs over the strong; the soft triumphs over the hard. No one in the world but knows this, yet no one can put it into practice.

This is why the Saint says: He who bears the reproach of the kingdom becomes the ruler of the kingdom.

He who bears the calamities of the kingdom becomes the king of the whole realm.

The words of truth seem contrary to reason.

Water is like the Way, says a commentator, because it can enter into all forms, and move in all directions. It bends or rises; it will fill a square vase as well as a round vase. If an obstacle blocks its way, it stops; if you open a passage for it, it will go wherever you desire. Yet it carries great ships, tears down rocks, hollows out valleys, pierces mountains, and upholds Heaven and earth.

Another commentator declares that the men of the world think that only the base will endure reproaches. But the Saint holds that they should be endured without complaint. If his words seem foolish and contrary to reason, this is only because they are judged from the point of view of the multitude.

79

Though you appease the great hostilities of men, they will still retain a residue of hatred.

How could they become virtuous?

Therefore the Saint keeps the left half of the contract and expects nothing from others.

This is why the virtuous man thinks of giving, and he who is without virtue thinks of asking.

Heaven is without predilection, and gives constantly to the virtuous.

The thoughtful Chinese commentators may be summed up thus: It is better to remain indifferent, and to forget equally the good which we have imparted and the injuries which we have received. Hostilities are born of illusion, and illusion springs from our nature. He who knows his nature, and keeps it pure, has no illusions; how should he feel hostility? But those who cannot tear up the root of hostility are able only to cut off the branches; therefore, though outwardly calm, they nurse hatred in their hearts. He who is perfectly sincere, has no conflicts with others. He lets them follow their natures and does not arouse their hostility; he gives to each what he desires, and asks nothing from anyone.

The contract is a tablet of wood which can be split in two. On this the agreement to pay or deliver a certain thing is written. He who is to pay or deliver the thing agreed on, keeps the left half of the tablet, and he who is to receive it keeps the right half. When the receiver presents himself, holding in his hand the right half of the tablet, and it is found that the two halves fit accurately together, the giver delivers the object of the contract without raising the smallest question as to the rights or the sincerity of the receiver. When Lao Tzu says that the Saint keeps the left half of the contract, he means that he asks nothing from anyone, and that he expects others to ask of him whatever they desire.

The Saint gives to others, and asks nothing in return. But Heaven gives to him constantly, loading him with gifts and blessings.

So far, the Eastern commentaries. A Western commentator would be inclined to point out the close resemblance between the thoughts of this most Christian of Orientals, born six centuries before Christ, and the words of the Master Christ; for example, the sentence quoted by Saint Paul:

"Remember the words of the Lord Jesus how he himself said, It is more blessed to give than to receive."[79]

It is the spirit of the Sermon on the Mount:

"I say unto you, Love your enemies, and pray for them that persecute you; that ye may be the sons of your Father which is in Heaven: for he maketh his sun to rise on the evil and the good, and sendeth rain on the just and the unjust. Ye therefore shall be perfect, as your heavenly Father is perfect."[80]

80

Had I a little kingdom with few inhabitants, if they had weapons for ten or for a
    hundred, they should not use them.
I should teach them to fear death and to remain at home.
If they had boats and chariots, they should not enter them.
If they had breastplates and spears,
    they should not equip themselves with them.
I should bring them back to the use of knotted cords for records.
They should eat their food with satisfaction,
    they should find their clothing pleasing,
    they should be satisfied with their dwellings,
    they should love simple customs.
Were there another kingdom so close to mine that the crowing of cocks and the
    barking of dogs could be heard from one to the other, my people should grow
    old and die without visiting the neighbouring people.

The Chinese commentators understand this eloquent little sermon in the sense of the
simple life and the age of gold. But it is more likely that Lao Tzu has in mind the life of
the disciple, which is indeed simplicity, a return to the golden age. Perhaps the most
illuminating parallel is this, from *Light on the Path*:

    "When the disciple has fully recognized that the very thought of individual
    rights is only the outcome of the venomous quality in himself, that it is the hiss of
    the snake of self which poisons with its sting his own life and the lives of those
    about him, then he is ready to take part in a yearly ceremony which is open to all
    neophytes who are prepared for it. All weapons of defence and offence are given up;
    all weapons of mind and heart, and brain, and spirit. Never again can another man
    be regarded as a person who can be criticized or condemned; never again can the
    neophyte raise his voice in self-defence or excuse. From that ceremony he returns
    into the world as helpless, as unprotected, as a new-born child. That, indeed, is
    what he is. He has begun to be born again on to the higher plane of life, that
    breezy and well-lit plateau from whence the eyes see intelligently and regard the
    world with a new insight."[81]

This is the site of Lao Tzu's "little kingdom," and this is the reason why those who
dwell there will not arm themselves with spear or breastplate, nor seek again to return to
"the other kingdom."

81

Honest words are not ornate; ornate words are not honest.
The man of worth is not glib of speech;
    the glib of speech is not a man of worth.
He who knows the Way is not erudite;
    he who is erudite knows not the Way.
The Saint lays not up treasure.

The more he spends himself for men, the greater grows his power.
The more he gives to men, the richer he becomes.
Such is the Way of Heaven, which lavishes blessings on all beings and harms none.
Such is the Way of the Saint, who toils, yet without contention.

True words, say the commentators, need no adornment. Who acts rightly needs no eloquence. Who possesses the heart of the matter need not be learned in many things. The Saint uses the Way for mankind, he gives all his treasures to men. Though he lavish his treasure on all the men of the kingdom and on ages to come, the Way grows ever greater for him, and is inexhaustible; his treasure ever increases and knows no diminution.

Heaven nourishes all beings, helping all and harming none. The Saint furthers the kingdom through the Way; when his works are fulfilled, he is detached from them. He seeks neither reward nor glory.

Here ends the Tao Te Ching

Notes

1. Logos (Greek λόγος), lit. "word" or "speech" in its mystic sense, also called the "Verbum of the Thought Divine," is a term used primarily in Greek philosophy, from the pre-socratic philosophers (see Heraclitus: "all things come to be in accordance with this Logos") to Plato and down to the Neoplatonists. The idea is greatly developed by Philo, for whom the Logos is the "Mind of God." From Philo, the idea made its way into Christian theology, through John, as the "Word of God"; see John 1:1: "Εν ἀρχῇ ἦν ὁ λόγος, καὶ ὁ λόγος ἦν πρὸς τὸν θεόν, καὶ θεὸς ἦν ὁ λόγος,"—"In the beginning was the Word (Logos), and the Word (Logos) was with God, and the Word (Logos) was God."

Johnston explains:

"John was not the originator of this expression: the Logos. It is generally admitted that he took it from Philo Judaeus (circa B.C. 20-A.D. 50) of Alexandria, who in turn found it used by the Stoics and Plato. ... In his philosophical, and we may add eminently theosophical writings, Philo develops the teaching of Plato, that all manifested things have their divine originals, their prototypes, which Plato called Ideas. Philo called these same divine originals, or principles, Logoi, and taught, with Plato, that the world-process consists in the orderly manifestation of these Logoi, under the forms of created things with which we are familiar. Philo further taught that these Logoi were summed up in a single collective Life, the host of the Logoi, to which, as a unity, he gave the name Logos. This collective Logos, Host of the divine Thought, stands above the manifested world, and through the Logos the eternal Deity works and becomes manifest." ("A Page of the Apocalypse", *Hidden Wisdom: Collected Writings of Charles Johnston* (2014))

While the term "Logos" is itself Greek, the idea it represents is found to have its equivalents in all major spiritual philosophies, both east and west, and, as Johnston points out, the equivalent in Chinese is *Tao*. Thus when the Christian bible is translated into Chinese, the term Logos is translated as Tao; the same verse as above in traditional Chinese (Union version) reads: "太初有道,道與神同在,道就是神"; "In the beginning was the Word (Tao), and the Word (Tao) was with God, and the Word (Tao) was God."

The Logos is a complex subject and is explored at length in Theosophical literature. See, in particular: H.P. Blavatsky, *The Secret Doctrine* (1888); *Transactions of the Blavatsky Lodge* (1890-91); and T. Subba Row, *Notes on the Bhagavad Gita* (1888). See also Johnston's translation and commentary of the *Bhagavad Gita*, the *Yoga Sutras*, and the *Mukhya Upanishads* for more on the Logos under is various guises.

2. John 15:22

3. Romans 8:7

4. *Bhagavad Gita*, II:57

5. Matthew 12:47-50

6. *Bhagavad Gita*, II:47-48

7. Vach (Sk.) is the mystic personification of speech, and the female Logos. Manu says that: "Having divided his body into two parts, the lord (Brahmā) became with the one half a male and with the other half a female; and in her [Vach] he created Viraj" (*Manu*, Sloka 34, book I.). Viraj may be termed "material Nature" with Vach as "Spiritual intelligent Nature." Vach has also been called the "manifested expression of the eternal divine Ideation." For more, see *Manu*, Book I., and *Vishnu Purana*, etc.

8. 1 Corinthians 1:24

9. Romans 1:20

10. *Crest-Jewel of Wisdom (Vivekachudamani)*, verse 78. See: Charles Johnston, *The Vedanta Philosophy of Sankaracharya* (2014).

11. Mabel Collins, *Light on the Path* (1885), Part I:16

12. *Ibid.* I:17 and II:19-21

13. *Brihad Aranyaka Upanishad*, IV:4:8

14. See Note 9.

15. *Bhagavad Gita*, VII:19

16. Mabel Collins, *Light on the Path* (1885), Comments, IV

17. John 14:6 and Matthew 11:29

18. *Bhagavad Gita*, VIII:14

19. Mabel Collins, *Light on the Path* (1885), Comments, IV

20. *Bhagavad Gita*, VI:20

21. *Katha Upanishad*, II:1

22. Second Rule of the Friars Minor, 6.

23. Isaiah 53:2

24. *Katha Upanishad*, I:2:3

25. Mabel Collins, *Light on the Path* (1885), Comments, IV

26. Prakriti (Sk.) is Nature in general, or "objective" or "material" nature, as opposed to Purusha, or "spiritual" nature. Prakriti is often translated simply as "matter" and Purusha as "spirit," thus the polar duality of spirit-matter pervading all manifestation. Together they have been referred to as the "two primeval aspects of the One Unknown Deity."

27. H.P. Blavatsky, *The Secret Doctrine* (1888), I:57.

28. Luke 4:16-22

29. Revelation 3:18-19

30. Ralph Waldo Emerson, "Circles", *Essays: First Series* (1841)

31. Mabel Collins, *Light on the Path* (1885), Comments, IV

32. Isaiah 53:3, 7, 11-12

33. Matthew 5:38-42. The Sermon on the Mount spans Matthew 5-7.

34. The Greek term is ἀντιστῆναι (antistínai).

35. For more on this subject, see: *Hidden Wisdom: Collected Writings of Charles Johnston* (2014), "Pre-Historic Wisdom."

36. See note 26.

37. *Prashna Upanishad*, VI:5

38. *Brihad Aranyaka Upanishad*, III:8:9

39. Mabel Collins, *Light on the Path* (1885), II:20-21

40. *Brihad Aranyaka Upanishad*, IV:4:7

41. 1 Corinthians 15:31

42. Mabel Collins, *Light on the Path* (1885), Comments, II

43. *Bhagavad Gita*, V:10, 12

44. Matthew 5:20

45. Luke 15:7

46. Mabel Collins, *Light on the Path* (1885), I:21

47. 1 Corinthians 15:43

48. 2 Corinthians 12:9

49. 2 Corinthians 13:4

50. See note 7.

51. Matthew 23:12

52. Matthew 11:29

53. See the "Parable of the Hidden Treasure" and the "Parable of the Pearl" (Matthew 13:44-46).

54. The "heart within" is a term used throughout the Upanishads. See, for instance: *Chhandogya Upanishad*, III:14:2-4 & VIII:1:3; *Taittiriya Upanishad*, I:6; *Brihad Aranyaka Upanishad*, IV:4:22; etc.

55. *Katha Upanishad*, I:3:3-4

56. *Brihad Aranyaka Upanishad*, IV:4:22

57. *Isha Upanishad*, 4

58. Mabel Collins, *Light on the Path* (1885), Karma

59. Matthew 5:43-45, 48

60. Mabel Collins, *Light on the Path* (1885), Part I

61. John 10:8

62. Matthew 7:24

63. John 3:3, 5

64. *Bhagavad Gita*, IV:38

65. Thomas Dekker, *The Honest Whore* (1604), Part I, Act V. Scene II:
> Patience, my lord. Why, 'tis the soul of peace.
> Of all the virtues 'tis near'st kin to heaven.
> It makes men look like gods; the best of men
> That e'er wore earth about him was a sufferer,
> A soft, meek, patient, humble, tranquil spirit,
> The first true gentleman that ever breath'd.

66. Matthew 12:19-20

67. *Tao Te Ching*, 5

68. Matthew 8:27

69. Matthew 23:12, Luke 14:11, Luke 18:14

70. Philippians 2:6-9

71. Matthew 9:13

72. John 12:25

73. In an article titled "The Kingdom of Heaven and the Upanishads", *The Open Court*, December, 1905, Johnston explains: "In the phrase: 'he that loveth his life,' the Greek word *psyche* is used, a word which seems to cover one great idea in the New Testament, but whose identity is veiled under several different English words. The same is true of the derived adjective *psychikos*. For instance, *psychike* is translated 'sensual' in the verse 'this wisdom descendeth not from above, but is earthly, sensual, devilish.' (James 3:15) ... There are two realms of our life, beside the mere physical body. There is a psychical body, and there is a spiritual body. The psychical body is the realm of the passions and desires, of all selfish and self-seeking impulses, of which Paul himself has given such full and vigorous lists again and again. Those who live in the psychical body, with no sense of anything higher, he calls 'the dead,' as in the phrase 'to be carnally minded is death'; (Romans, 8:6) or in the words, 'you who were dead in trespasses and sins.' (Ephesians, 2:1) And the most complete worldly success would still leave its possessor numbered among the 'dead' in this sense. Paul then conceives a quickening of the life from above, or 'a birth from above'."

74. Mabel Collins, *Light on the Path* (1885), II:1

75. *Ibid.*, I:18

76. *Ibid.*, I:16

77. Maya (Sk.) is typically translated as "illusion." In his commentary upon the *Katha Upanishad*, Johnston refers to Maya as "the great Illusion of Differentiation." In commenting upon Gaudapada's *Mandukya-Karika*, he echoes Sankaracharya's illustrations of Maya:

> "A rope is lying on the ground; a man, seeing it indistinctly, believes it to be a snake. So is the world of illusion perceived in the Real. But there is no snake there at all; so it cannot be said to have a beginning, nor can it be said to come to an end. It simply does not exist. So is it with the illusion of a world of pain, separate from the Divine. Again, the world-illusion is like the robber imagined by the belated wayfarer, who sees a post in the twilight. When he sees that it is really a post, and no robber, it cannot be said that the robber has come to an end. There simply was no robber. So also with the mirage, the lake fancied in the salt desert ..."

Maya has been elsewhere called "the cosmic power which renders phenomenal existence and the perceptions thereof possible."

78. See: Matthew 10:39 & 16:25, Mark 8:35, Luke 9:24.

79. Acts 20:35

80. Matthew 5:44-45, 48

81. Mabel Collins, *Light on the Path* (1885), Comments, IV

Books by Charles Johnston

The Tao Te Ching: Lao Tzu's Book of the Way and of Righteousness, 1st Edition (2016). ISBN: 978-1537196473.

The Bhagavad Gita: Songs of the Master, 2nd (Expanded) Edition (2014). ISBN: 978-1490451404.

The Yoga Sutras of Patanjali: The Book of the Spiritual Man, 3rd (Expanded) Edition (2014). ISBN: 978-1484926635.

The Vedanta Philosophy of Sankaracharya, 1st Edition (2014). ISBN: 978-1495946691

The Mukhya Upanishads: Books of Hidden Wisdom, 1st Edition (2014). ISBN: 978-1495946530.

Hidden Wisdom: Collected Writings of Charles Johnston (2014), 4 vols.

The System of the Vedanta, Dr. Paul Deussen, tr. Charles Johnston, 1st Edition (1912). ISBN: 978-1519117786

Essays and Article Collections by Johnston

Karma: Works and Wisdom

The Memory of Past Births

The Theosophy of the Upanishads

Wisdom Traditions of East and West

The Noble Teachings of Lord Buddha

Unveiling the Wisdom of the Bible

Emanation & States of Consciousness

The Beginning of Real Life

On Initiation and the Mysteries

The Logos Doctrine

A Study of Ancient Speech and Writing

Collected Writings

http://www.universaltheosophy.com/writings-johnston/

Made in the USA
Columbia, SC
26 February 2018